June ac Bartlett

D1537997

June ac Bartlett

EVERYDAY COLLECTABLES

SPORTING PASTIMES

EVERYDAY COLLECTABLES

SPORTING PASTIMES

WHSMITH
EXCLUSIVE · BOOKS ·

Editor Dorothea Hall
Art Editor Gordon Robertson
Production Craig Chubb

Concept, design and production by
Marshall Cavendish Books
58 Old Compton Street
London W1V 5PA

Produced exclusively for W H Smith Limited
by Marshall Cavendish Books Limited

© Marshall Cavendish Limited 1990

All rights reserved. No part of this publication may be reproduced, stored in a retrieval system or transmitted in
any form or by any means electronic, mechanical, photocopying, recording or otherwise, without the prior
permission of the publishers and the copyright holder.

Typeset by Litho Link Ltd., Welshpool, Powys, Wales
Printed and bound by Dai Nippon, Hong Kong

ISBN 1 85435 321 7

CONTENTS

INTRODUCTION

In an age when sport attracts both participants and spectators in ever increasing numbers, it is fascinating – and rewarding in every sense – to look back at times when there was no film, television or video coverage to foster enthusiasm for such events and yet they attracted great support.

It was also a period when technological developments were beginning to produce more sophisticated equipment to increase the player's scope, when women's fashions at last enabled them to participate more freely, and when the introduction of the bicycle made a day in the country possible for even the less well-to-do.

Sporting Pastimes covers all these aspects and an astonishingly rich and attractive variety of collectables – for both indoor and outdoor activities – from playing cards and chess pieces to the cricket bat, golfing accessories and even guns, swords and daggers.

For both the Victorians and the Edwardians, sporting pastimes tended to be seasonal activities (no world tours and international events on today's scale to extend the enjoyment), but as well as golf, tennis and cricket, they included fishing, hunting and shooting. Around this time artists produced a wealth of drawings, paintings and watercolours recording sporting activities, now very much prized by collectors – especially the sporting prints which are now enjoying a massive revival in popularity.

Indoor leisure pastimes also receive due coverage, and there are many attractive collectables in this sphere, from the humble cigarette cards – which look very impressive now when a full complement of, say, sporting personalities or famous international racers is mounted within a frame – to playing cards and beautifully crafted chess pieces that are as decorative as they are usable. Also of high ornamental value are the skillfully carved and lifelike decoy ducks, and even items such as binoculars are often as handsome as they are usable.

So, the scope for collectors, whatever their interest in sport, is as wide as it could possibly be. This highly illustrated book provides a memorable visual insight into the immense range of sporting antiques that are still widely available today – and the authoritative accompanying text is as informative as it is readable. Each piece is discussed in detail and there is much advice on what to look for, how to assess quality and craftsmanship, recognize leading makers' marks (invaluable in dating a piece), and to differentiate between the genuine and clever fakes.

There is also excellent back-up in the form of price guides to help you evaluate pieces for your collection and thus avoid paying excessive prices. However, it should always be borne in mind that prices do vary depending on the part of the country where you make your purchase, its general condition and, of course, rarity value. Also, fashions change – as in all things – and what was deemed desirable becomes less so, only to resurface again some years later – as indeed taxidermy has. With that proviso, professional antique dealers rely on price guides such as the ones printed here, and they certainly are safeguards against unwise investments, so do consider them carefully. (See the Price Guide below for the key to the price codes used within the book.)

Enjoy the book, enjoy the hunt for 'finds' and, of course enjoy using or displaying them – knowing that you have also made a sound investment.

Tony Curtis

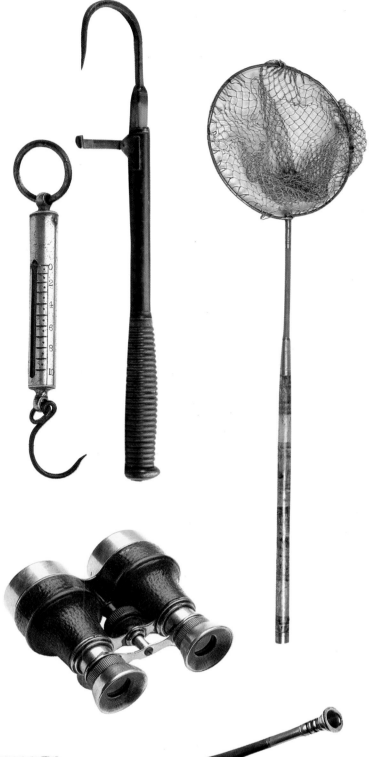

Ogden's Cigarettes.

GALOPIN.

PRICE GUIDE	
KEY	❺ £150–£300
❶ £10–£20	❻ £300–£600
❷ £20–£40	❼ £600–£1400
❸ £40–£80	❽ £1400–£6000
❹ £80–£150	❾ £6,000 plus

Victorian Country Study

Taking on different guises from office to private den, the Victorian
gentleman's study was a room which most strongly reflected its owner's
tastes – including his many hobbies and pastimes

The Victorian study was a snug and intimate room that is still much imitated today. Then, as now, the most vital ingredient of the study was the influence of its owner, whose work, hobbies and pursuits the room reflected. Unlike present day versions, however, it was a male domain.

The study in a Victorian country house was decorated and equipped in a typically practical and rather busy Victorian style. Primarily centred around the owner's estate business, its furniture would include a desk, sensible chairs and probably a drum table. But the room would also reflect his interest in country sports, with rods and guns on the wall, and rather less formal pieces of furniture such as a chest for fishing flies and a herbarium cupboard.

Above all, however, the study was a room for relaxation and reading, and this was very much reflected in its decor. The fire was constantly lit, the chairs were comfortable, and the walls were lined with favourite books and paintings.

The study/library at Flintham House, Newark, Nottinghamshire which was added by the Victorian architect, T. C. Hine, in 1851.

◀ *The secluded atmosphere of his own private study provided the wealthy Victorian country gentleman with the desired comfort amid surroundings which bore the mark of his personality. Here, while partaking of morning refreshment, he could conduct his business affairs without being disturbed by the activities in the rest of the house.*

▼ *Many Victorian country studies had to house purely functional furniture where estate files and papers were kept but the room still retained all the trappings of comfort, including a well-padded armchair and favourite books. The owner's collection of sporting prints, paintings showing hunting scenes and several of his hunt trophies frequently adorned the walls of his study.*

To the Victorian country gentleman, the study was a place from which to carry out the running of the estate and the pursuit of his hobbies. It was very much his private retreat, not be be entered without his express permission. It was also, emphatically, part of the male domain within the house, a domain that also included the billiard and smoking rooms.

THE MALE DOMAIN

The division of the house into male and female portions evolved from the Georgian practice of ladies and gentlemen going to separate rooms for after-dinner conversation. The early Victorian years had been strongly religious times, in which the emphasis was very much upon the family and husbands and wives spent a great deal of time together. But by the later, more secular years of the Queen's reign, the separation of the sexes was in full swing, so much so that husbands and wives scarcely met, other than at dinner or bedtime!

OFFICE, DEN AND JUSTICE ROOM

In many ways the study was the male counterpart to the lady of the house's boudoir, and would often even have an adjacent dressing room and its own WC.

Although the largest, longest-established country houses would often have separate rooms for the library, office and the gentleman's relaxation room,

elsewhere the study was often used for a combination of these purposes and hence equipped with books, desk and chairs as well as the trappings of comfort. Perhaps it is not surprising, therefore, that it enjoyed more than a few alternative names, being variously referred to as the business room, the office, or the den. It was sometimes also called the justice room, because English Justices of the Peace could hear cases in their own homes until 1848, and the study was invariably the place where such proceedings took place. It was also the room where the country estate owner might mete out justice to miscreants such as poachers.

The study was usually near to either the main entrance to the house or the entrance to the servants' wing – it would never do for ordinary visitors such as estate tenants of any sort to tread the hallowed halls of the Victorian gentleman's house.

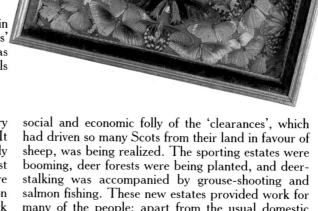

◀ *The growing interest among many Victorians in their countryside's rich fauna and flora generated new hobbies, one of them being the preservation of moths and butterflies. The most attractive specimens were pinned down to form beautiful patterns in contrasting colours and framed behind glass to decorate the walls of the gentleman's study.*

COUNTRY LIFE

The Victorian age was the great period of country house building in Britain, especially in Scotland. It was a time when the middle classes were really beginning to come into their own, and the wealthiest – great industrialists and men of commerce – were buying country estates and building fine houses on them. There they would escape from the 'dark satanic mills' – which might well have brought them their fortunes – and enjoy the country life, country air, hunting, shooting and fishing. In Scotland, the social and economic folly of the 'clearances', which had driven so many Scots from their land in favour of sheep, was being realized. The sporting estates were booming, deer forests were being planted, and deer-stalking was accompanied by grouse-shooting and salmon fishing. These new estates provided work for many of the people; apart from the usual domestic staff, there was a need for ghillies and gamekeepers to look after the sporting side of the estate.

Staff were particularly important, since the owner

Town and Country

LEAVING BEHIND THOSE 'DARK SATANIC MILLS' AND THE BIG INDUSTRIAL TOWNS WHICH BRED THEM, MANY WEALTHY VICTORIANS REDISCOVERED NATURE IN THEIR OWN WAYS AND INVESTED THEIR NEWLY-MADE CAPITAL IN BIG COUNTRY ESTATES WHERE THEY AND THEIR FAMILIES COULD ENJOY A MUCH HEALTHIER LIFE. THE GROWING INTEREST IN THE COUNTRYSIDE ALSO SAW THE FOUNDING OF NATURE SOCIETIES AND A MULTITUDE OF BOOKS WRITTEN ON THE SUBJECT.

THE 19TH CENTURY WAS A TIME OF EXPLORATION AND DISCOVERY, NOT JUST OF DISTANT PLACES, BUT ALSO OF SCIENCE AND NATURAL HISTORY. THE SWEDISH SCIENTIST LINNAEUS HAD BY NOW DEVELOPED HIS BINOMIAL SYSTEM OF NAMING PLANTS AND ANIMALS; AND THROUGH CLASSIFICATION, THE NATURAL WORLD COULD BE SEEN TO HAVE ORDER AND PATTERN. CHARLES DARWIN SHONE A LIGHT NOT JUST ON THE PRESENT STATE OF NATURE BUT ON ITS WHOLE DIM HISTORY WITH HIS IDEA OF EVOLUTION. MEANWHILE THE INDUSTRIAL AGE WAS IN FULL SWING; THE SMOKY, NOISY FACTORIES WERE INCREASINGLY THE SOURCE OF THE NATION'S WEALTH, AND THE GREAT CITIES WERE EXPANDING RAPIDLY. THOSE WEALTHY ENOUGH TO DO SO SOUGHT ESCAPE IN THE COUNTRY. IT WAS INEVITABLE, THEREFORE, THAT THE VICTORIAN COUNTRY GENTLEMAN SHOULD HAVE A STRONG INTEREST IN THE NATURAL WORLD AROUND HIM, AND IN HIS PLACE IN IT. THE WRITINGS OF SUCH AS DICKENS AND T. H. HUXLEY WERE BEGINNING TO LEAD TO THE IMPROVEMENT OF THE LOT OF PEOPLE IN THE GRIMY HELL OF THE INDUSTRIAL CITIES AND SOME OF THE GREATEST WRITERS ON THE NATURAL WORLD – W. H. HUDSON, RICHARD JEFFERIES AND GILBERT WHITE – WERE LAYING THE FOUNDATIONS OF THE CONSERVATION MOVEMENT OF THE 20TH CENTURY.

▲ *On the days when the country squire could absent himself from his official duties, one of his delights might have been to go partridge shooting in the grounds of his own estate, accompanied by his ghillie and faithful hunting dogs.*

of the estate might not always be there; many of the new Scottish lairds, for example, were prosperous English businessmen who spent much of their time further south. But when the owner was in residence, the study was at the heart of his affairs.

STUDY FURNISHINGS

The Victorian country study would contain a desk, probably at the window – a fine, heavy desk accompanied by typical mid-Victorian drawing-room upright chairs, for, as one contemporary put it, 'it is impossible to write on rickety chairs at a shaky table'. Here paperwork such as accounts and estate management papers would be kept, though rent books might well be placed in a drum table in alphabetically labelled drawers. The desk would have inkstands, in which the ink would be kept free and clean, and not allowed to become dry, thick or dirty. Beside the inkstand was a blotter, which was regularly replaced when it became ragged.

For comfort, by the fire was a favourite winged chair, usually with an antimacassar draped over the back to protect the surface from the macassar oil on the gentleman's hair. Next to the chair was a round table with a few favourite books on it. On the hearth were cushions for the faithful old gundog, and the fire was kept lit, even when the room was not in use, not least to ensure that mildew was kept from the books which occupied the bookshelves that lined at least two of the walls. Again to avoid damp and mildew, these shelves would start above floor level.

Like many of his contemporaries, the Victorian gentleman was interested in the natural world, and among the atlases and bound copies of *Punch* on the shelves would be found works on natural history and the countryside – local flora, perhaps – and, say, Watson's *Topographical Botany* or Halford's *Dry*

◄ *A decanter cabinet could often be found among the paraphernalia in the study: a cupboard-like stand made of oak or mahogany, it contained a gentleman's favourite whisky and smoking accessories.*

◀ *Pride and joy of the dedicated country gentleman was his gun. This example is a 19th-century air gun made of plain stock with engraved steel mounts. The spherical reservoir near the trigger was pumped up with air before shooting.*

LIFE AND LEISURE

Victorian Desk Lamps

RE-CREATING THE FEEL OF A VICTORIAN COUNTRY STUDY CAN EASILY BE ACHIEVED WITH CAREFULLY CHOSEN FURNITURE AND FITTINGS. A DESK, COMPLETE WITH PEN, INKSTAND AND BLOTTER, IS ESSENTIAL, AND LIBRARY BOOKSHELVES LADEN WITH LEATHER OR BUCKRAM-BOUND BOOKS WILL ADD TO THE ATMOSPHERE. ROOM MAY BE FOUND ON THE WALLS FOR SOME SPORTING OR EQUESTRIAN PRINTS.

IN THE EVENINGS, THE DESK WOULD HAVE BEEN ILLUMINATED WITH A POOL OF LIGHT FROM A SMALL DESK LAMP. THIS WOULD PROBABLY HAVE BEEN AN OIL LAMP AS ELECTRIC LIGHTING WAS NOT YET COMMON IN THE COUNTRY.

OIL LAMPS WERE OF ORNATE WELL-POLISHED BRASS AND FROSTED GLASS – THOUGH SOME HAD A CERAMIC RE-SERVOIR FOR THE OIL, WHICH WOULD HAVE BEEN KEROSENE, WHALE OIL OR COLZA, WHICH WAS MADE FROM KALE. 'STUDENT' LAMPS, WHICH WERE DOU-BLE LAMPS ON A SINGLE STAND, WERE ESPECIALLY POPULAR.

GENUINE AND REPRODUCTION VIC-TORIAN TABLE LAMPS ARE AVAILABLE FROM ANTIQUE DEALERS AND FROM LIGHTING SPECIALISTS.

Fly Entomology. A line dryer – for silken fishing lines – might well be clamped to the bookshelf.

On the walls rested favourite trout and salmon rods, and perhaps a gun or two, and in the corner of the room were a butterfly net and killing bottle – the means with which the fine selection of pinned and set butterflies and moths, mounted in a glass-topped case, had been captured and put to rest. Much of the remaining space on the wall would be filled with sporting prints of hare-coursing, pheasant-shooting and fox-hunting. If the owner was a racing man there would be prints, too, of outstanding racehorses, though, naturally, some space was reserved for oil paintings of the family, a map of the estate and the crowning glory of the room – a proudly displayed stuffed salmon, which the owner had caught himself in the river which flowed through the estate.

The walls themselves were decorated with wall-paper or panelled wood, which was considered to be very masculine. On the floor was a large Turkey rug or a patterned carpet, while the windows were draped with heavy winter curtains which would be replaced by lighter ones in summer.

In the corner of the room was a mahogany chest containing a selection of salmon and trout flies, and nearby was a large safe – or the door to an adjoining strong room – which housed the most important estate papers and the family records.

AT THE END OF THE DAY

When the work was done, this snug little room was a place for relaxation, a purpose for which it was more than adequately equipped. On the wall was a piperack, and on a heavy side table behind the sofa stood a tantalus, Cut-glass whisky tumblers on a plain silver tray and a soda water siphon; the latter, in those days, would typically have a string bag around it. An oil lamp for reading was generally kept on the table.

When it was time for bed, the Victorian country gentleman would leave his study to ascend the private staircase which led to his wife's boudoir and the family bedroom; the study and these rooms often comprised what amounted to a private suite on two floors. He could now rest, having dealt with the day's running of a busy estate and perhaps look forward to spending the next day out of the study. In the morning he would take his salmon rod down from the study wall, select some brightly coloured fishing flies from the chest and go forth with his ghillie to enjoy a fine day's fishing – a pleasure which fully justified to him the cost and labours of running a Victorian country estate.

The Salmon Fly

Fly fishing was a favourite pursuit of many Victorian sporting gentlemen,
who took great pride in their collection of tackle and often displayed it
proudly in the study

Well-to-do gentlemen of the latter decades of the 19th century spent a considerable amount of time in the pursuit of game. Activities which had attracted the sporting eye in the early part of the century – bare-knuckle prizefighting, bull-baiting and the like – were giving way to country sports such as fox-hunting, deer-stalking, pheasant and grouse shooting and, most popular of all, fishing.

VICTORIAN ANGLERS

For Victorian gentlemen, from Prince Albert downwards, the spring and summer months were the time to enjoy the skills and pleasures of fly fishing – the tempting of trout and other game fish to their fate with artificial lures resembling waterside and aquatic insects.

Angling appealed to the Victorians because it was healthy and sporting, and because, all being well, it would end up with the gentleman asserting human superiority over nature by outwitting, capturing and killing his quarry. It was also enjoyable, as Mr Halford, the author of *Dry Fly Entomology* admitted in 1897: 'Of course, there is a certain charm about it; the most lovely time of year, the long days, the continual excitement and the out-of-door life all tending to make a sort of picnic'.

In the chalk streams of southern England, trout would be the angler's favoured prey. But the owners of the great and burgeoning sporting estates north of the border, and their guests, might have a greater challenge on their minds – namely the capture of the leaping, shining salmon on their way upstream to their spawning grounds. The salmon was king in the lochs and silver streams of the Scottish estates, and the landowner's fishing rights were treasured.

▲ *The country gentleman seen here in Scotland is accompanied by his two ghillies, who would help him carry the equipment to the river and hopefully carry back the day's catch. Salmon fishing was very popular in Victorian times, not least because the salmon was 'the monarch and king of the fishes'. Special fishing methods had been introduced to catch this elusive fish, which so often managed to eject the hook or break the line and escape.*

The angler might order his fishing wardrobe from the 'Country Gentleman's Catalogue', where, amongst the manure carts, thrashing machines and steam boilers, could be found a section on angling equipment, including brogues, waders, rubber boots, stockings and hats.

A DAY'S FISHING

When ready, he would summon his ghillie, who was then, as he is now, indispensable to a successful day's salmon fishing. Companion, advisor and helper, he would have been a local man, retained as part of the estate workforce, who knew the waters and the fish of the estate intimately.

On the ghillie's advice, the gentleman chose the stretch of water he would fish that day. It might well have been a lively reach plunging and splashing across a distant hill on the grouse moor to then fall into a deep, still pool.

They would approach the water gently and slowly so as not to disturb the fish, perhaps crawling the last few yards across the damp open ground so as not to shadow the water. A fly would be selected to suit the conditions, and the ghillie would prescribe where best to cast – a fish might be visible in the clear water, or he might know a place were a salmon might lie hidden. A series of accurate casts would present the lure to the salmon, and eventually there would be a bite. Hooked, the salmon would run and leap from the water and the angler would play it, until finally the king of the river would tire and be landed. If the fish was a particularly fine specimen, it might be stuffed and proudly mounted in the study.

FLIES AND LURES

Great skill was involved in making the elaborate fishing flies used to attract the unwary salmon. Waxed silken thread was used to assemble feathers and fur on to a hook so that the whole resembled an insect, either on the water's surface (a dry fly), or beneath it (a wet fly).

Salmon flies are best regarded as lures since salmon do not feed after leaving the sea to return upstream to spawn. The fish will take them, although why they should do so is a mystery. In the main, Victorian anglers used the wet fly to bait salmon, since the dry fly was thought to be less effective.

For trout, the right fly was chosen, or tied on the

◀ *Wet salmon flies were often a prized possession of the fisherman. They were kept in a wallet or tin to protect the dressings from being crushed. Stored in neat rows, the many different patterns and sizes would be displayed so the gentleman could select the most appropriate fly. From its humble beginnings in 1725, the salmon fly had evolved into a highly decorative piece, often consisting of up to 30 different materials to create its visual effect.*

THESE DOUBLE-HOOKED FLIES HAVE METAL EYES, WHICH WERE INVENTED IN 1845 AND IN GENERAL USE BY 1890.

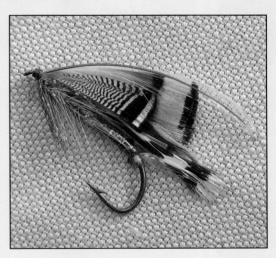

A SINGLE HOOK, OR IRON, WHICH DISPLAYS THE DETAIL OF MATERIALS AND COLOURS USED TO MAKE THE FLIES.

A SINGLE- AND DOUBLE-HOOKED FLY, WITH THE MORE TRADITIONAL GUT EYE THAT WAS USED IN VICTORIAN TIMES.

◀ *'Brook Trout Fishing—An Anxious Moment' is the title of this picture dated 1862. The fish has taken the fly but, as always, it requires the angler's skill with rod and reel to land the fish.*

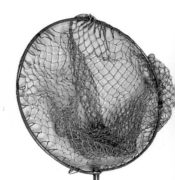

spot, to resemble as closely as possible the insect that the fish appeared to be taking at the time.

The Victorians took the construction of fishing flies very seriously. In order to produce exactly the right shape, size and colours, a great range of materials was needed. Feathers came from birds as varied as the black cock, bird-of-paradise and condor. Animal fur was also important, often coming from a particular part of the body – such as behind a hare's ear. Even rat's whiskers were used – to imitate the tails of a mayfly. To get the colours right, the raw materials were dyed using concoctions made from ingredients such as bark, extract of indigo or the brown outer leaves of an onion. The finished materials could then be used to create such romantically named flies as Flight's Fancy, Summer Duck, Pale Olive Quill and Claret Smut.

The long and careful process of tying required a tool kit including a small pair of forceps, a dapping needle for teasing out feathers and fur and probably a small vice for holding the hook during tying.

Few flies survive from before Victorian times, and even late 19th-century ones are not particularly common. They were, after all, not regarded as items to be kept. When a fly became too worn, the most serviceable parts were removed and used again, whilst the rest was discarded. An angler would usually expect a fly to last a season at best.

RODS AND REELS

The angler went to the water armed with a range of equipment designed to help him trap his quarry. Rod designs had become quite sophisticated and by the 1880s, robust and very flexible tropical woods like greenhart were coming into use, replacing local woods. Split cane rods were also popular. In one issue of the 'Country Gentleman's Catalogue' Hardy's of Alnwick advertised their rods with a

recommendation from Prince Albert, who expressed his 'complete satisfaction' with their cane-built steel centre rod. Hardy's were also the leading manufacturer of fishing reels. With a fine rod, a well-made reel, a silken line and his flies, the angler was well equipped for his day's sport.

Although it is said that the great fish of the Victorian era have gone – netted at sea or in the estuaries – salmon fishing is still as popular and exciting as it always was. And for fly fishermen away from the salmon rivers, more and more waters are being stocked with trout, so there is ample opportunity to cast the wet or dry fly today.

▷ PRICE GUIDE ▷   ANGLING ANTIQUES

Victorian angling antiques are becoming increasingly popular not only with fishing enthusiasts but also because of their fine craftsmanship.

▲ *This brass and cording landing net, dated 1880, is both attractive and practical. The telescopic cane handle can be detached from the net.*

PRICE GUIDE ❹

◀ *Wooden salmon reels were the most common types at the end of the 19th century. The ivory-handled brass reel is earlier.*

PRICE GUIDE ❺

▶ *The metal fly tyer's vice (top) is late Victorian, as is the fly tyer's pricker with cherry wood handle. The needle was used for pricking out the eyes.*

PRICE GUIDE ❸ ❺

◀ *This late Victorian split reed creel, bound in leather, is in near perfect condition and therefore expensive. It was often used to hold spare tackle. The brown leather and canvas waders date from the same period.*

PRICE GUIDE ❻ ❸

▲ *A leather fly wallet c. 1900 containing gut-eyed flies. The wallet usually held the angler's personal selection of traditional fly patterns.*

PRICE GUIDE ❺

▼ *A hand-crafted brass fish scale dating from the late 19th century. The measures, numbered up to ten, are in pound weights.*

PRICE GUIDE ❸

▼ *Mid to late Victorian fishing rods in different woods, bamboo and cane.*

PRICE GUIDE ❺

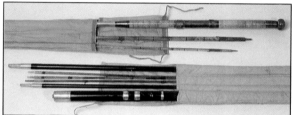

▼ *A salmon landing gaff in brass and rosewood c. 1860. The banded handle makes it easier to hold on to.*

PRICE GUIDE ❹

Poaching

EVER SINCE THE DAYS WHEN KINGS, LORDS AND LANDOWNERS CLAIMED OWNERSHIP OF GAME, THERE HAVE BEEN POACHERS. SOME STOLE FISH AND FOWL IN ORDER THAT THEIR FAMILIES DID NOT STARVE, OTHERS TOOK THEM FOR PROFIT. DURING THE 19TH CENTURY, THE PENALTIES FOR POACHING WERE EXTREMELY SEVERE AND, WHILE TRANSPORTATION, OR EVEN DEATH, WAS THE PUNISHMENT FOR BEING CAUGHT, THE POACHER MIGHT BE CAUGHT IN A TRAP LAID FOR HIM. DESPITE THESE DISINCENTIVES, TROUT WERE TICKLED, PIKE CAUGHT WITH POLE AND NOOSE, AND SALMON NETTED. ONE OF THE MOST FAMOUS SALMON POACHING STORIES CONCERNS A POACHER ON THE RIVER EARN, WHO CAUGHT A SALMON OF 102 POUNDS — AN ABSOLUTELY HUGE SPECIMEN. HE COULD NEVER SHOW OFF HIS CATCH, THOUGH, SINCE HE HAD CAUGHT IT ILLEGALLY AND AFTER IT HAD BEEN WEIGHED HE HAD NO OPTION BUT TO CUT IT UP AND SELL IT!

▶ POACHERS IN SCOTLAND, DEPICTED BY THE 19TH-CENTURY PAINTER, JAMES WINGATE.

Guns

Technical developments improved guns of all kinds in the Victorian and Edwardian eras: many were attractively finished providing added appeal to the collector

The invention of the percussion cap at the beginning of the 19th century revolutionized the manufacture of guns. This was a small charge encased in a copper cap which, when struck by the gun's hammer, caused a flash to pass down the 'nipple' into the powder. Unlike the flintlock firing mechanism of earlier guns, it was unaffected by the weather. It was also much faster in its action and far less likely to misfire.

The result was a boom in the manufacture of sporting guns from the 1820s onwards. They ranged in quality from the finest Joe Manton, at 60 guineas, down to a poor £1 gun for shooting vermin. Manton went bankrupt, but the two greatest names in gun-making of this period had both worked for him at one time. They were James Purdey and Charles Lancaster.

The best guns had Damascus barrels forged from twisted rods of alternate iron and steel, locks of forged iron and steel filings, and stocks of Circassian walnut. Increasingly they came in fine mahogany cases lined with baize and with compartments for loading and cleaning equipment. Cheap guns had locks made from die-stamped components, stocks of beech stained to imitate walnut, and barrels

manufactured from 'sham damn skelp' – the poorest scrap. They were all, of course, muzzle-loaders.

PERCUSSION RIFLES

Guns that fire shot have smooth barrels, those that fire bullets are rifled – that is, they have a spiral groove inside the barrel that imparts a spin to the projectile, giving extra accuracy. The first percussion rifle to be issued to the British army was the Brunswick rifle in 1838. It had a 30in (75cm) barrel and deep two-groove rifling designed for firing a ball with a raised broad belt that fitted into the grooves. The Brunswick was accurate, but its problem was that after a few shots the rifling in the barrel became fouled with burnt powder, and loading was difficult.

The Minié Rifled Musket of 1851 was a great improvement. It fired an elongated lead bullet which was easily loaded, and which expanded when fired to give a gas-tight fit. The Enfield rifle, developed for use in the Crimea, followed this principle, but the invention of the brass-cased, breech-loading bullet in 1865 made Minié's system obsolete. The new metal-cased bullet was fired by the famous Martini-Henry rifle adopted by the army in 1871. Later

improvements included the bolt action of the Enfield Mark 1.

Rifles were not so popular for sporting use in Britain as on the Continent, but their greater range, accuracy and power made them ideal for deer hunting. And when big game hunting became fashionable in Asia and Africa they proved an indispensable weapon. The design of 19th-century British sporting rifles was based on the German Jäger rifle.

The other great change in gun design in

COMPARISONS

Big Game Rifle

A RARE DOUBLE-BARRELLED RIFLE, CUSTOM-MADE IN 1884 FOR HIS HIGHNESS IZAM HYDERABAD, WHO WAS THEN THE WEALTHIEST MAN IN THE WORLD. THE FURNITURE AND BARRELS ARE DECORATED WITH GOLD TOOLING.

the 19th century has already been mentioned. It was the breech-loader. The Frenchman Le Faucheux patented a breech-loader shotgun in 1835, but it didn't catch on in Britain until after it was shown at the Great Exhibition of 1851.

NEW AMMUNITION

The new kind of gun required a new kind of ammunition. Gone were the powder, wadding and shot of the muzzle-loader, and the cartridge made its appearance. Joseph Lang was the first British manufacturer of the pinfire breech-loader. This held a cartridge with a protruding pin, which the hammer drove into the cartridge, firing the gun. There was also a rimfire cartridge which was fired by being struck on the rim. But in 1861 George Daw produced the first centrefire cartridge, which has scarcely changed to this day.

In the 1880s steel began to replace Damascus in barrel manufacture. And by

▲ Published in 1874, this etching by Henry Alken shows Frank Raby 'flapper shooting'. Then as now, the double-barrelled shotgun was the most popular weapon for field sports as it allowed two shots at a fast-moving target. The spray of shot from each cartridge might also down more than one bird.

the end of the century, hammerless and ejector guns had appeared as well as breech-loaders, that could fire more than one cartridge without reloading – the forerunners, in fact, of the modern automatic rifle.

ADVENT OF THE REVOLVER

Between the 1820s and the 1840s a large number of multiple-barrelled pistols were made. They were known as pepperboxes and were the forerunners of the revolver. The first really efficient revolver, with a single barrel and revolving multiple chamber, was patented in 1836 in America by Samuel Colt. The Colt Peacemaker became one of the most popular handguns of the American West, used by lawmen and outlaws alike. 'God did not make all men equal,' the saying went, 'but Colt's revolver did.'

In 1853 Colt built a factory in Pimlico, London, and in the four years of its existence it produced 50,000 of his guns. British gunmakers were not slow to take up the challenge, and soon began producing revolvers of their own. Tranter, Westley Richards, Adams and Webley were the main manufaturers.

Initially the revolver was a single-action weapon, and had to be cocked each time it was fired. But with the double-action revolver, one squeeze of the trigger both cocked and fired the gun, making possible many of the bloodier episodes of the Wild West.

Britain in the 19th century was a rather less lawless place. Duelling had died out. Highwaymen were a thing of the past. There was no longer the necessity to carry guns for personal protection. The possession of guns was therefore confined largely to those who shot for sport, to gamekeepers who shot vermin and to the military.

◄ A fine cased set of antique target or duelling pistols. Made in 1850 by Fauré-Lepage, they are in a velvet-lined case with all their accessories. Within the case can be seen a brass bullet mould. In front of the case are a ramrod, copper percussion caps, lead ballshot and a powder flask.

▲ A rare pair of rifled percussion pocket pistols, made by H. Holland in about 1842. The complete set of tools, in an oak box, includes a barrel spanner.

PRICE GUIDE **8**

▼ A .41 calibre, rimfire pistol with over-and-under barrels. Made by Remmington in 1892, it fitted a waistcoat pocket and was popular with Mississippi gamblers.

PRICE GUIDE **6**

◄ A .41 calibre, rimfire Colt Derringer, made in 1878. It has a spur trigger, wooden hand-grip and a barrel that swings out for loading. The frame is nickel-plated.

PRICE GUIDE **5**

► A 6-shot, pinfire pepperbox revolver. Made by Perrez of Belgium in 1870, it has a black grip and chambers. The folding trigger allows it to fit neatly into a case.

PRICE GUIDE **6**

◄ Very similar to the pepperbox above, this 6-shot gun has rusted a little due to lack of care. It has an ivory grip and decoratively engraved metalwork. Fitting into a purse or pocket, pepperboxes were especially popular with the ladies.

PRICE GUIDE **6**

Handguns

The duelling pistol of the 18th century developed into the target pistol of the 19th century. These percussion pistols were rifled for greater accuracy and came in cased pairs that were often lavishly equipped. French and Belgian pistols were deeply carved all over with Gothic fantasies, and their accessories were similarly finished and laid out in compartments of velvet or gold-tooled leather.

British target pistols were elegant in shape and decorated with fine scroll engraving. They were made by several leading British gunmakers including James Purdey. The gunmakers' best work was often out of sight, in the rifling of the barrel, the inside of the lock, and in the set trigger mechanism, which needed the merest touch to fire the pistol.

Pepperboxes were weapons for personal defence, and were mostly functional rather than beautiful. Some, however, were finely finished and engraved in silver. They came in velvet-lined cases with bullet mould, nipple key, powder flask, cleaning rod, spare nipples and a tin of percussion caps.

The Colt is probably still the most prized revolver for the collector. The other major manufacturers in the USA were Remmington and Smith & Wesson, who went into partnership in 1854 and produced the first revolver to use the metallic-rim cartridge which was later adopted by Colt.

British revolvers were usually sold in oak cases with compartments for accessories. As well as the trade label on the lid, these sometimes still contain instructions for use.

The automatic pistol, which superseded the revolver, was developed at the turn of the century. The leading makes were the German Luger and Mauser and the British Webley.

PRICE GUIDE

▶ A .31 calibre, Colt pocket percussion revolver. This is the 1849 model, made in the USA. It has an underlever rammer, brass trigger guard and wooden hand-grip. It comes complete with its tools in the original box, with directions for cleaning.

PRICE GUIDE **8**

▲ A .38 calibre, black powder, 5-shot centrefire revolver. It has scroll engraving and a gilded finish. It was made in 1887 by J. M. Marlin of New Haven, Connecticut.

PRICE GUIDE **5**

▼ The legendary Colt 45 Peacemaker, with which the West was won. It is a single-action army revolver with an ivory handle. Patented in 1871, this particular gun was made in 1880.

PRICE GUIDE **7**

◀ A Colt .22 calibre, rimfire, open frame revolver. It has a wooden grip and was an ideal lady's or waistcoat gun. It was made in Hartford, Connecticut in 1878.

PRICE GUIDE **5**

▶ A Colt .35 calibre, semi-automatic, pocket pistol. A spare magazine, which held 6-shots, is shown alongside. It was sold in a red leather and purple velvet case. Automatics took over from revolvers and could be inconspicuously carried in town.

PRICE GUIDE **5**

PRICE GUIDE

Long-barrelled guns

The carbine had a shorter barrel than the musket or rifle, and was issued to the cavalry as well as to light infantry, light dragoons and the artillery. The Winchester repeater carbine is famous as the saddle weapon of the U.S. cavalry. In Britain the move towards breech-loading military weapons resulted in the Westley Richards carbine. This was nicknamed 'the monkey tail' because of the lever arm which lifted from the top of the grip to open the breech. It was approved as the official cavalry firearm in 1861.

The blunderbuss has always been attractive to collectors. When it was used as a weapon to protect the home it had to be kept permanently charged and primed. Its traditional position over the fireplace has a practical origin in that the heat from the fireplace served to keep the powder dry.

Percussion blunderbusses continued to be made in the 19th century. The barrels and non-mechanical parts (the furniture) were usually brass. Contrary to what one might expect, the shot didn't actually leave that great bell-like mouth with any greater spread than if the barrel had been cylindrical. But no doubt the big bell muzzle had a considerable deterrent value.

The British gun trade of the 19th century was centred on Birmingham, and few people bought guns from abroad. The best hunting or Jäger rifles were made in Germany. The leading gunsmith was Christoph Funk of Suhl.

▲ A breech-loading, Martini, action service carbine. Made in Europe in 1877, this particular gun was used in Muscat and has Arabic lettering on the engraved metalwork.

PRICE GUIDE ④

▲ A rare 40 bore, percussion, transitional rifle, with a spur hammer firing mechanism and revolving chambers. Made by H. Holland in 1845, it has an octagonal barrel and a pistol grip.

PRICE GUIDE ⑧

▲ A double-barrelled, 10 bore, black powder ball gun, made by Holland & Holland in 1878. Designed to be fired from an elephant's howdah, it has short barrels and a rare double action, firing pinfire and centrefire cartridges.

PRICE GUIDE ⑨

PRICE GUIDE

▲ A Colt Lightning, slide-action, sporting rifle of .38-.40 calibre. Notice the wooden pump-action beneath the barrel. The rifle retains much of its original finish, it was made in 1896.

PRICE GUIDE **7**

▲ A military, breech-loading, 450 bore rifle, nicknamed 'the monkey tail'. It was made by Westley Richards and has a brass trigger guard and collapsible sight.

PRICE GUIDE **6**

▲ Made in 1912 by F. W. Kessler of Suhl in Germany, this is an 8mm single-shot deer rifle. The stock and action are engraved with hunting scenes and the fluted steel barrel is inlaid with silver. The gun has a set trigger.

PRICE GUIDE **8**

PRICE GUIDE

COLLECTOR'S TIPS

The new collector of guns would do well to begin with a reliable dealer or a visit to a respectable auction room. Bargains may occasionally be found on the stalls, but so may fakes, so try and learn as much as you can by reading before you decide to buy.

There are plenty of possible areas in which to specialize. The quaintly made pepperbox multi-barrelled pistols are always popular. Another area to consider is 19th-century sporting percussion guns and rifles, as these are often overlooked in favour of more expensive 18th-century flint-lock fowling pieces or military weapons.

Single-barrelled shotguns were used principally by farmers to shoot vermin and meat for the pot, rather than by sportsmen, so good quality examples tend to be rarer than with double-barrelled guns. Again the lighter British sporting rifles – known as 'rook-and-rabbit' guns – are quite rare, because shotguns were usually used for such small game. American ones, however, are common.

In Britain the size of a gun is expressed as a numbered bore. A '12 bore' is a gun that fires a lead ball, weighing 12 to a pound. The ball actually measures .747 of an inch in diameter, so in America such a gun would be called a '.747'.

WHAT TO LOOK FOR

The quality of a gun can be judged by its balance, its graceful lines and the fit and finish of its parts. The quantity of engraving is no guide at all, but restrained, high-quality engraving is usually the mark of a good gun. Guns bearing the name of one of the best makers are especially collectable. The proof marks with which guns were stamped are not an indication of quality.

Long-barrelled Pistols

DECORATIVE DETAILS DO NOT NECESSARILY MAKE A GUN MORE VALUABLE. THE PLAIN SINGLE-SHOT, BB RIMFIRE SALOON PISTOL IS WORTH A LITTLE MORE THAN THE 250 BORE, SINGLE-SHOT, TARGET PISTOL AT THE TOP.

Cased Colt Revolver

THIS IS THE .36 CALIBRE, COLT NAVY PERCUSSION REVOLVER. MEASURING 12INS (30CM) OVERALL, IT HAS A 6½IN (16CM) OCTAGONAL BARREL. THE CHAMBERS HOLD FIVE SHOTS AND FIRE EITHER LEAD BULLETS OR SPHERICAL LEAD SHOT. MADE IN 1856, IT IS A RELATIVELY EARLY REVOLVER AND IS A SINGLE-ACTION WEAPON THAT HAS TO BE COCKED EACH TIME IT IS FIRED.

① THE UNDERLEVER RAMMER FOR CLEARING THE CHAMBERS.

② BULLET MOULD FOR MAKING ONE'S OWN LEAD BALLSHOT AND BULLETS. (MOLTEN LEAD IS POURED INTO THE TOP OF THE CLOSED MOULD).

③ A TIN OF PERCUSSION CAPS MADE BY ELEY BROS FOR COLT.

④ A BAG-SHAPED POWDER FLASK WITH A GRADUATED BRASS NOZZLE.

⑤ WOODEN BOX CONTAINING SPARE STRIKING PINS.

⑥ LEAD SHOT.

·CLOSE UP·

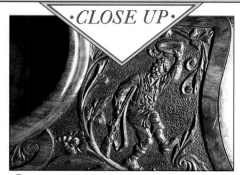

① CARVED STOCK

② ENGRAVED ACTION

③ PROOF MARKS AND 'MONKEY TAIL'

④ PEPPERBOX CHAMBERS

⑤ MAKER'S MARK

ADDRESS. COL. COLT. LONDON

⑥ DOUBLE-ACTION HAMMERS

① A VERY DECORATIVE CARVED WOODEN STOCK ON A GERMAN DEER RIFLE, SHOWING A HUNTER IN LEDERHOSEN AND PLUMED HAT AMONG SCROLL MOTIFS.

② METAL ENGRAVING ON THE ACTION OF A DEER RIFLE. THIS SCENE DEPICTS HINDS AND A FAWN. ON THE OPPOSITE SIDE IS A BELLOWING STAG STANDING BY ONE THAT HAS BEEN SHOT.

③ THE STAMPED PROOF MARKS INDICATE THAT THE GUN HAS BEEN PROOF-FIRED AND PASSED SAFE FOR USE. THE LEVER ARM WAS KNOWN AS 'THE MONKEY TAIL'.

④ THE BUSINESS END OF A 6-SHOT PEPPERBOX REVOLVER, SHOWING THE 6 NOTCHED CHAMBERS. THERE WAS NO SINGLE BARREL IN FRONT OF THE CHAMBERS.

⑤ THE TELEGRAPHIC ADDRESS FOR COLT'S LONDON FACTORY, PIMLICO, STAMPED ON THE TOP OF A RIFLE BARREL. MOST MAJOR GUNSMITHS MARKED THEIR WORK.

⑥ DOLPHIN-SHAPED, DOUBLE-ACTION HAMMERS THAT WERE SET UP TO FIRE BOTH PINFIRE AND CENTREFIRE CARTRIDGES. ALL THE METALWORK IS FINELY ENGRAVED.

They simply show that the gun was proof-fired before finishing and was passed safe to use.

When examining an antique gun, check the stock for splitting or woodworm. Check the barrel for rust and lifting inlay. Remember that cocking an antique gun can break a weak main spring, and above all remember that it could be loaded.

CLEANING AND DISPLAY

Rust can be removed from old guns using 0000 steel wool soaked in light oil. For stubborn patches scrape with a copper coin which won't scratch the surface. Stocks can be cleaned with the same fine gauge steel wool soaked in meths. Afterwards rub in a coat of boiled linseed oil.

You can remove barrels and locks from the gun for cleaning purposes, but don't try to dismantle the lock. This is a job for an expert. When you've finished cleaning, wipe the gun to remove finger marks, or better still wear cotton gloves throughout — the salts in your skin can corrode the metal. Avoid overcleaning and remember that the rust may hide some decoration, so don't damage it by being over enthusiastic with the oil-soaked steel wool when refurbishing.

The best place to display guns is in a glass-fronted case which protects them from dust. Long guns should be stored pointing downwards to prevent oil staining the stocks. Heat and damp will both damage weapons, so don't store them over a fire or an exterior wall.

Guns that are kept as collectors' pieces must be a hundred years old before they're excluded from the need for the relevant firearms certificate, and you must have a shotgun licence if you have a shotgun that can be fired. But the laws are currently under review, so try to keep abreast of any changes that could affect you as a collector.

REAL OR FAKE?

Guns were finished in a particular way in the 19th century and one of the ways to spot a fake is to examine the finish carefully. The barrels were browned with nitric acid and mercury sublimate to prevent rust. The furniture — trigger-guards, butt plates, ramrod pipes and so on — was heated in charcoal dust to blue it; locks were colour-hardened by baking in bone dust and old shoe soles.

■ Original barrel brown should have a delicate, greyish tinge.
■ Charcoal blue has the iridescence of a peacock's feather.
■ Colour-hardening produces blues, browns and greys somewhat reminiscent of a thunder-laden sky.

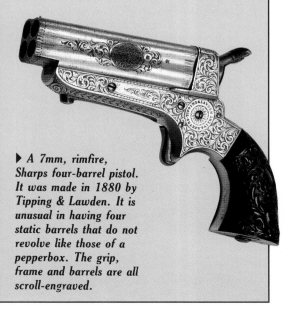

▶ A 7mm, rimfire, Sharps four-barrel pistol. It was made in 1880 by Tipping & Lawden. It is unusual in having four static barrels that do not revolve like those of a pepperbox. The grip, frame and barrels are all scroll-engraved.

The Sporting Print

From Georgian to early Victorian times the robust, unrestrained life of daredevil country sportsmen was captured in sporting prints which were as popular in the 19th century as they are today

By the end of the 19th century the sporting print was fondly regarded as a memory of a bygone age. Many of the 'sports', such as dog fighting and bull baiting, were already things of the past. The late Victorians, who saw their own world as less picturesque and less humorous, were much taken by the vivacity and madcap behaviour in sporting prints from the Georgian and Regency periods, and in country houses many now adorned the walls of a gentleman's study.

HEYDAY OF THE SPORTING PRINT
The English sporting print dates from around 1770. It was perfected between 1800 and 1850, fading away with the onset of new reproduction processes and the consequent decline of the master engraver's art after 1870. During the hundred years of its popularity the sporting print produced a unique record of the life of the hunting, fishing and racing country squires. These landowners rode to hounds, showed off their skills as horsemen, delighted in the challenge of driving a fast coach and seemed prepared to take on anything for a wager.

COMPARISONS

Early or Late?

FIRST IMPRESSIONS — FROM THE FIRST EDITION OF 100 OR 200 PRINTS — HAVE THE FINEST DETAIL. LATE IMPRESSIONS, WHEN THE PLATE HAS WORN, HAVE A WASHED-OUT LOOK.

A LATE IMPRESSION. THE BLACK HORSE HAS BECOME GREY AND ITS MANE HAS BEEN CRUDELY TOUCHED UP.

A FIRST IMPRESSION. THE AQUATINT GROUND IS STRONG, THE COLOURS ARE GOOD AND LINES ARE UNBROKEN.

Colonel Thomas Thornton, a celebrated country character and sportsman from Yorkshire, patronized Sawrey Gilpin, an artist who soon earned good money for his sporting works. Thornton was a falconer, hunter, shooter and a great gambler and in the 1790s there was a great demand for depictions of the Colonel's exploits.

ARTISTS AND ENGRAVERS

Working from their original painting, some artists personally etched or engraved the plate from which prints of the work were produced. Often, however, much or all of the plate-making was left to a master engraver. The best of these engravers became as well known as the artists.

John Scott, who died in 1828, was one of the early, expert line engravers. When engraving a large print after a major artist, such as Sawrey Gilpin, it would be in his hands for up to six years.

Though animal painting had long been popular, it was the work of George Stubbs on the anatomy of the horse that really stimulated the accurate treatment of sporting subjects after 1766. An excellent artist, he also experimented widely with engraving techniques. His son, George Townly Stubbs, continued the family tradition, engraving many of his father's paintings.

Thomas Gooch was another artist who improved the fidelity of representation in sporting pictures. He produced a set of six paintings, entitled 'The life and death of a racehorse', which were exhibited at the Royal Academy in 1783 and published as aquatint prints in 1790.

Thomas Rowlandson, at his best from 1780 to 1790, was not primarily a sporting artist but produced several pictures on sporting themes which were reproduced as prints. Despite their popularity, he was penniless and forgotten by the time of his death in 1827. He also engraved other artists' work.

James Pollard was one of the most highly valued artists, with his fishing scenes and coaching prints especially in demand. He was soon better known for engravings after his works than for his original paintings – which included such unexpected subjects as 'Lioness attacking the Exeter Coach', an event which actually happened when a lion escaped from a travelling menagerie!

The celebrated Henry Alken's work spanned the period of the best sporting prints published by Rudolph Ackermann, Thomas McLean and S & J Fuller. His

◀ The print stand was useful for storing unframed prints. The print of the racehorse Diamond is from a stipple engraving (c. 1820) by John Whessell, after a painting by the prolific sporting artist, John M. Sartorius. The framed print is by the aquatint engraver John Harris III from a painting by Henry T. Alken.

early pictures were signed 'Ben Tally-Ho' and showed mainly steeplechases and hunting scenes. His son, Henry Gordon Alken, had a good but inferior talent, often passing off his own paintings as his father's.

Another father and son combination began with Dean Wolstenholme, who was second in popularity only to Alken. He produced hunting, coursing and shooting scenes after 1803. Dean junior engraved both his own and his father's pictures.

The last of the old school of sporting artists was Charles Cooper Henderson who died in 1877 – by then the reign of the popular sporting print was almost at an end.

SUBJECTS OF THE PRINTS

The commemoration of notorious bets soon established itself as a popular subject for the sporting print. As early as 1788 a print was produced to immortalize a wager involving the speed and endurance of the Duke of Queensbury's horse-drawn carriage. The print sold for 1 guinea, in colour, or 10s 6d in black ink.

The great five-mile race between 'Clinker' and 'Clasher', for a bet of £1,000, was similarly recorded. So also was the run of the mare Nonpareil, which trotted 100 miles in ten hours.

'Squire' Osbaldeston, Master of the Quorn Hunt and a successful jockey who was frequently painted by Henry Alken, won his 1,000 guinea bet that he could ride 200 miles in nine hours at Newmarket – a feat duly recorded in a print.

▲ A fine example of a stipple engraving by George Townly Stubbs after a painting by his father, George Stubbs. It was published in London by the father-and-son team in 1794. Today it is very much a collector's piece, valued at around £2,000.

The exploits of John Mytton – said to be half mad without drink and quite mad with it – featured in many Alken prints. Another character recorded because of his amazing feats was Captain Basby, who was reputedly able to stand an 18-stone man on his right hand and lift him onto a table.

A bet involving a rat-catching dog inspired another print. 'Billie', the dog, and his owner had both lost an eye in their ratting experiences, but the dog happily set to to kill 100 rats in 12 minutes in a 12-foot square pit.

Such colourful characters and events gave endless scope to the popular artists, but it was hunting – beagles and harriers after hares, hounds after the fox – shooting and fishing that really dominated the art. Horse racing, the stagecoach and the mails were equally popular subjects. Coaching scenes, especially deep in the winter snows, were great favourites and still have an irresistible attraction.

Today, these sporting prints, with their detailed backgrounds and closely observed people, give a fascinating insight into a vanished age – an age recorded for posterity by the combined talents of the artists and engravers of the day.

Horse Prints

In a tradition which continues today, racehorse owners commissioned portraits of their thoroughbreds. Prints were made of the famous winners of the classic races and these were eagerly snapped up by the racing fraternity.

In the days before newspaper photographs and television, it was left to the artist to capture the great moments in racing history. Stirring finishes were depicted by painters and the ensuing prints were much in demand. Famous exploits in the hunting field were similarly recorded and the names of the most notorious riders and horses were often included beneath the print.

In these action prints, however, the artists' abilities were stretched by the necessity to depict horses in a rapid movement which deceived the eye. The animals' bodies barely clear the ground and their legs are stretched to an impossible reach.

Even dogs appear in the stretched, low-slung 'rocking horse' pose which now seems so artificial, though nonetheless charming. It would seem likely that the artists were following convention rather than trying to accurately depict movement.

A beneficiary of George Stubbs' pioneering work on the anatomy of the horse was John Frederick Herring (1795-1865) of Doncaster. He painted portraits of many winning racehorses. His works, which are much admired today, were engraved by various professionals, including Thomas Sutherland and Richard Gilson Reeve.

Henry Thomas Alken (1785-1851) was the most noted artist and engraver of action-packed racing and hunting scenes. These were engraved by himself and others.

One of four prints from a set entitled 'The First Steeple-Chace on Record'. This is a reprint published by Ben Brooks.

PRICE GUIDE 4

'The Fox Chase', an aquatint by the eminent engraver Charles Hunt I after F. C. Turner. Complete with a poem, it was published in 1834.

PRICE GUIDE 5

PRICE GUIDE

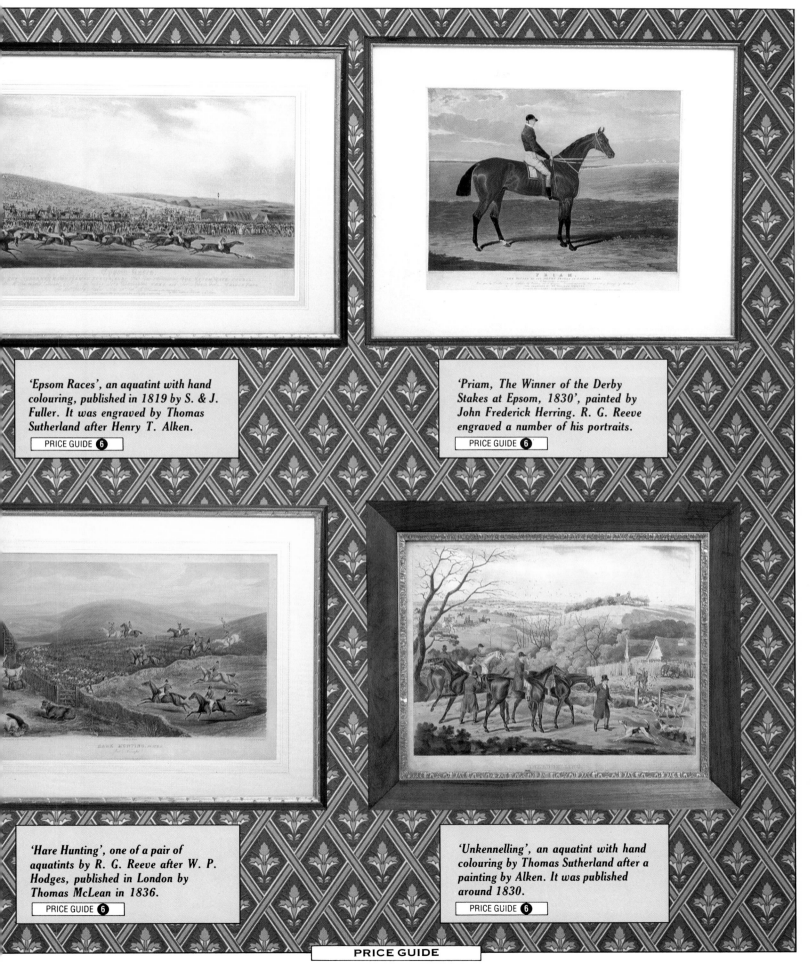

'Epsom Races', an aquatint with hand colouring, published in 1819 by S. & J. Fuller. It was engraved by Thomas Sutherland after Henry T. Alken.

PRICE GUIDE **6**

'Priam, The Winner of the Derby Stakes at Epsom, 1830', painted by John Frederick Herring. R. G. Reeve engraved a number of his portraits.

PRICE GUIDE **6**

'Hare Hunting', one of a pair of aquatints by R. G. Reeve after W. P. Hodges, published in London by Thomas McLean in 1836.

PRICE GUIDE **6**

'Unkennelling', an aquatint with hand colouring by Thomas Sutherland after a painting by Alken. It was published around 1830.

PRICE GUIDE **6**

PRICE GUIDE

Coaching and Country Sports

The leading artist and engraver of coaching prints was James Pollard (1797-1867). Others, such as the Rosenbergs and John Harris III, engraved many of his later paintings.

Fishing and shooting scenes are very popular. George Morland painted a number of these in the 18th century and his works were engraved by, among others, Samuel Alken, George Keating and Thomas Rowlandson. Samuel Howitt was perhaps the most prolific engraver of these subjects, executing 72 plates for his 'The British Sportsman' series.

Bull baiting, cock fighting and other brutal sports are out of favour and can be bought at attractive prices.

▶ *Coaching prints have long been popular. Near right is 'The Red Rover, Southampton Coach', an aquatint engraved by Charles Hunt and published around 1830. Far right is 'Loosing 'Em', one of a pair of coloured lithographs published about 1880.*

PRICE GUIDE **7** **6**

▼ *'Royal Cock Pit', aquatinted by John Bluck after an illustration by Thomas Rowlandson and A. C. Pugin. It was published in 1808.*

PRICE GUIDE **5**

▼ *'Bull Baiting', one of 50 plates from The National Sports of Great Britain, published in 1820.*

PRICE GUIDE **2**

▶ *Portrait of a terrier named 'Crab', by Clark after Alken. This is an aquatint in which the colours have been printed, not added by hand.*

PRICE GUIDE **5**

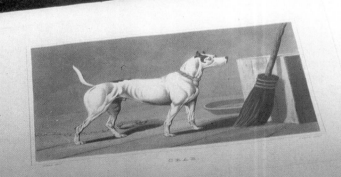

▶ A hand-coloured print entitled
'The Shannon Side', engraved by
Edward Hacker after H. L. Rolfe.

PRICE GUIDE **3**

▲ The way colour lithography
could mimic crayon is shown by
this picture of 'Barbel Fishing',
printed about 1840.

PRICE GUIDE **4**

COLLECTOR'S TIPS

In pure metal engraving the whole design is carved into the plate using a fine chisel known as a burin. By the 18th century, however, etching had become the printmaker's principal technique. Acid took the place of the burin, eating into the plate to produce the indentations which held the ink during printing. The copper plate was first covered in acid-resistant wax and the wax was then scratched away in the required design. The plate was immersed in acid and, where the wax had been removed, the acid would bite into the copper.

The engraver's burin was nonetheless still used to produce strong foreground details. The printmaker's craftsmen continued to be known as engravers and the prints they produced – largely by etching – are still sold today as 'engravings'.

The etching process was developed to produce many effects. Soft-ground etching involved adding tallow to the wax, giving a soft-edged line which, when printed, reproduced the effect of a pencil drawing.

◀ *'Barefoot', one of several classic racehorse portraits engraved by Thomas Sutherland after J. F. Herring in the 1820s.*

Stubbs' Prints

GEORGE STUBBS (1724-1806) IS BEST KNOWN FOR HIS ILLUSTRATIONS OF HORSES. TO MAKE THE 18 PLATES FOR HIS BOOK, *THE ANATOMY OF THE HORSE,* HE STUDIED HORSES IN DETAIL. DURING THE LAST YEARS OF THE 18TH CENTURY HIS EXPERIMENTS IN PLATEMAKING SET STANDARDS FOR THE FUTURE.

HIS SON, GEORGE TOWNLY STUBBS, ENGRAVED MANY OF HIS FATHER'S PAINTINGS, GENERALLY USING STIPPLE AND LINE. GOOD CRAFTSMAN THOUGH HE WAS, HIS ENGRAVINGS ARE LESS VALUABLE THAN THOSE OF HIS FATHER. THE PRINTS WERE PUBLISHED BY MESSRS STUBBS; OTHER PUBLISHERS REPRINTED THEM.

① MOST OF THE PRINT IS IN STIPPLE WITH SOME LINE WORK.

② BY TRADITION THE ARTIST'S NAME IS SHOWN AT BOTTOM LEFT.

③ THIS IS AN 1817 REPRINT, PUBLISHED BY EDWARD ORME.

④ THE ENGRAVER'S NAME IS USUALLY SHOWN AT BOTTOM RIGHT.

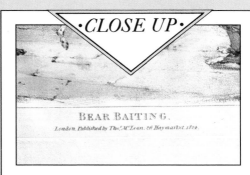

·CLOSE UP·

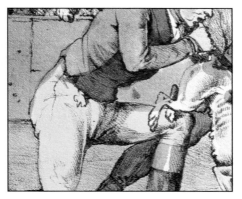

① **TITLE AND PUBLISHER**

① THE TITLE, PUBLISHER'S NAME AND ADDRESS WERE PRINTED CENTRALLY.

② THE INITIALS REFER TO A CATALOGUE WHICH HAS DATA ABOUT THE ARTIST.

③ ARTISTS' HAND-COLOURING IS LESS PRECISE THAN PRINTED COLOURS.

④ FLIMSY INDIA PAPER HOLDS THE FINEST DETAIL. DURING PRINTING IT WAS GLUED TO A BACKING SHEET WHICH SHOWS THE PLATE MARK.

⑤ THE MOTTLED GROUND OF AN AQUATINT. THE MEDIUM WAS SO CALLED BECAUSE IT RESEMBLES A WATERCOLOUR WASH. AQUATINTS CAN BE BLACK ONLY.

② **PRINTSELLERS' ASSOCIATION STAMP**

③ **HAND-COLOURING**

④ **INDIA PAPER AND PLATE MARK**

⑤ **AQUATINT GROUND**

THE AQUATINT

The development of aquatint gave a great impetus to the production of top-quality prints. The wax ground on the copper was porous – usually it was a mixture of resin and alcohol – allowing acid to percolate through it. The minute cracks in the resin were etched by the acid, giving a faint tone over the plate. It was possible to combine this with sharp and soft etched lines, producing a variety of sophisticated effects.

THE LITHOGRAPH

Lithography was also used for sporting prints. The finished effect looks rather like soft-ground etching but a glance at the edge of the print will distinguish between the two. An etching required considerable pressure in the printing press and the edge of the plate marked the paper; a lithograph has no such indentation. To produce a lithograph the image was drawn onto a moistened limestone slab with a greasy chalk; ink adhered only to the grease and not the wet areas, enabling a design to be printed.

Hand colouring of prints was a major endeavour. Artists who could produce flawless colours and delicate washes would have been in great demand. Hand-coloured prints have black outlines and textures beneath the colours. Later prints, in which the colours were separately printed by using a different printing plate for each one, have none of the black beneath, except where additional colours have been added by the hand colourist.

TOP QUALITY PRINTS

Many of the best prints were produced in sets sold between sheets of protective paper – such mint condition sets soon becoming very rare. First edition, unfaded prints are now exceptional. Only those that were carefully framed and hung in rooms where they were unlikely to fade in strong sunlight, or which were bound into books, have retained their original colours.

The most sought-after prints are the artist's early proofs and first impression prints from the initial print run. The plate became worn, especially if it was copper, after the first hundred or so prints. Plates were, however, retouched and reprints were run off but these usually suffer from a noticeable lack of detail.

POINTS TO WATCH

■ Early prints have the name and date on the picture and a publication line at the bottom, the date of which should be close to the date of the original painting.

■ Prints in the first half of the 19th century were made on Wove paper, showing no lines or watermarks other than a name – usually Whatman paper – and date on each sheet. Small prints may have used part of the sheet without such information.

■ It was a legal requirement that the print should show the name and address of the publisher. If the edge of the plate is marked by an indentation in the paper, but there is no publication line, then a reprint should be suspected. The line should only be missing if it has actually been cut off.

Detail from a Stubbs, showing stipple.

The Stirrup Cup

Made of pottery, porcelain and silver, the Victorian stirrup cup played a vital part in the ritual of fox-hunting. Shaped into an animal's head, the cups make decorative display pieces

Replete from a hearty meal in the breakfast room, members of the hunt gathered at the meet. This was held outside a local hostelry or inn or in the village market place. Alternatively, a wealthy landowner held a 'lawn' meet on the gravel sweep of his grand residence. Dressed in vivid scarlet or black coats, the riders received a short but potent drink from the stirrup cup.

THE RITUAL OF THE CUP

In the mid-Victorian era, the stirrup cup, shaped like the head of a fox or hound, was passed between hunt members by servants of the host's house. The cup was usually filled with a warming liqueur such as cherry brandy, Jamaica rum, or might contain a hot, potent punch.

It was passed first to the Master of Fox Hounds, then to the Huntsman, who is traditionally the next most senior hunt officer. The whipper-in and noblest guests among the hunt followers were next in line, and, finally, it circulated around the other riders. On the larger hunts, a tray of glasses was passed round,

or several stirrup cups, which sometimes belonged to a small set, though most cups were only made and sold in pairs.

EARLY MATERIALS AND DESIGNS

The stirrup cup derived from a simple glass or earthenware cup, which was handed up to horsemen arriving at a residence after a journey. The earliest mention of it in literature is in 1681 in a book by Thomas Flatman, called *Heraclitus Ridens*. He writes: 'Let's have one stirrup cup of character; it's the only modish liqueur now.' In the 18th and 19th centuries, there are other references to it as a 'hearty' and 'potent' refreshment for horsemen and women.

The traditional hunting design, representing a fox's, or sometimes a hound's, head was introduced at the end of the 18th century. Skilled silversmiths first started to make them by hand in about 1760. After 1800 they were normally cast, but continued to be made in the same design.

The workmanship was in most cases of a high quality, with the fox fur made to look as realistic as

▲ *Before setting out to face the rigours in the field, hunting parties in Victorian times often assembled outside the local inn to receive fortification in the form of a warming, potent drink. This was frequently served in a stirrup cup, a drinking vessel specially made for this purpose.*

possible. The rim of the silver cup was represented by a collar. Before 1800, the cups often had an indented rim, on which inscriptions about the hunt were engraved.

The cup was hollow, funnel-shaped and capable of holding little more than a typical sherry glassful. On the outside the ears were laid flat to the head, though sometimes they were extruded and could be used as supports for the thumb and finger when drinking.

The cup had no handle or feet as it was passed from person to person by hand. For presentation purposes, some sets of silver stirrup cups were made with a stand designed to grace the display cupboards of Victorian dining and breakfast rooms.

EARTHENWARE AND PORCELAIN
In the last quarter of the 18th century, Staffordshire potteries started to make foxes' heads out of earthenware. At first these were quite crudely modelled and splashed in green glaze. Later versions were shallower in shape and enamelled in more naturalistic colours with a rim or collar area of green. Some of the foxes were earless and creamy-white with decorative olive-green markings. Staffordshire made many fox-head stirrup cups for the next 70 to 80 years. Unfortunately, it was very rare to put painter's marks on the cups and few can be attributed to individual craftsmen.

ALTERNATIVE SHAPES
Almost as popular as the fox-head cups, hounds' heads were introduced in the 19th century and some of these are more easily attributable. For example, Ralph Wood II from Burslem made light olive-green earthenware versions with a translucent glaze, and John Turner of Green Dock produced a number of cane-coloured versions, matt on the outside and glazed on the interior.

Minton, Coalport, Rockingham and Spode were producing various bone china hound-head stirrup cups in natural colourings. Staffordshire also made bone china examples in neutral tones such as dull white, black and grey, reddish or grey-brown.

Stirrup cups were also made to resemble animals denoting other forms of game or sport. These include the heads of deer, trout, hares, cockerels, bears, bull-dogs, setters and bull-terriers.

TRADITIONS OF THE HUNT
What are now so sought-after and prized by the collector were, in mid-Victorian times, a minor part of the ceremony of the great British chase. Oscar Wilde, the renowned satirist, called fox-hunting 'the uneatable pursued by the unspeakable'. But to the wealthy mid-Victorians, the hunt was an event that loomed large in the rural calendar.

Fox-hunting originally dates from the 17th century. At first it was tried as an adjunct to stag- and hare-hunting and not held in esteem. In fact, it only acquired status and popularity when Hugo Meynell

▲ *The hunt breakfast formed an important part of the Victorian hunt ritual. It provided the necessary sustenance for the vigorous ride ahead and also gave the participants an opportunity to discuss and carefully plan their manoeuvres on the field.*

Foxes and Hounds

THIS FINE FOX-HEAD STIRRUP CUP IN PORCELAIN IS NOTABLE FOR ITS NATURALISTIC IMAGE.

PRECIOUS SILVER GILT FOX-HEAD STIRRUP CUP MADE IN LONDON AT THE BEGINNING OF THE 19TH CENTURY.

A QUITE CRUDELY MODELLED STAFFORDSHIRE HOUND'S HEAD WITH TYPICAL GREEN COLLAR.

HUNTING ACCESSORIES

Interesting items of Victorian hunting equipment can be picked up quite reasonably on antique market stalls. It is worth going to specialized dealers for more unusual pieces, but expect to pay higher prices.

◀ *Both these stirrup cups came out of Staffordshire potteries – using Portobello (above) and Prattware (below) designs.*

PRICE GUIDE **6**

▲ *A copper hunting horn, beautifully finished with a contrasting silver mouthpiece.*

PRICE GUIDE **3**

▶ *This soft grooming brush with walnut wood back could today be used as a clothes brush.*

PRICE GUIDE **4**

of Quorndon Hall in Leicestershire started hunting in the early 19th century. By the middle of the century, landowners and country gentlemen, along with many wealthier tenant farmers, met to hunt three or four times a week during the season. Fox-hunting is even reckoned to be responsible for making many gentlemen farmers and landowners interested in the welfare and upkeep of their country estates, which for generations had been neglected.

THE HUNT BREAKFAST

Ranking high on the list of elaborate Victorian hunt rituals was the hunt breakfast. This varied in style according to the hosts and guests of the day. Most people who attended had breakfasted at home before they left. 'Gentlemen', therefore, tended just to nibble at the spread, whereas farmers, who had breakfasted at dawn, were ready for a hearty meal and tucked in with relish. In general, however, etiquette demanded that the host provided plenty of food for his guests.

Between 40 and 100 guests took over the Great Hall in larger residences or the billiard or dining room in relatively smaller houses. In the book *Party-giving on every Scale,* dating from 1882, the hunt breakfast is described as 'partaking of the character of a cold luncheon on a large scale.'

A typical breakfast started at 9.30 am and involved a great many cold meats – large joints of sirloin or corned beef, cold roast pheasant or game pie, roast chicken or turkey – and a good quantity of cheese, normally a cheddar. By way of liquid refreshment sherry, brandy, cherry brandy, liqueurs and ale were always provided, and very occasionally champagne was also supplied. In one of his novels about countryfolk and their customs, Robert Smith Surtees gives us this account of a hunt breakfast table:

'. . . *in the centre stood a magnificent uncut ham,*

▲ *The side-saddle iron was designed to help Victorian ladies stay firm in the saddle.*

PRICE GUIDE **3**

Hunting Brews

IT WAS A MATTER OF PRIDE TO THE HOST THAT HIS GUESTS WERE WELL ENTERTAINED, AND CARE IN PREPARATION CERTAINLY EXTENDED TO THE CONTENTS OF THE CUP. HOWEVER, EXACTLY WHAT WAS CONTAINED IN A STIRRUP CUP WAS OFTEN THE SECRET OF HIS BUTLER OR HEAD SERVANT.

QUITE A COMMON DRAM OR 'GLASS' WAS A CHERRY BRANDY AND PORT MIX. ANOTHER FAVOURITE CONSISTED OF PORT AND HOMEMADE GINGER WINE, MIXED FIVE PARTS TO ONE.

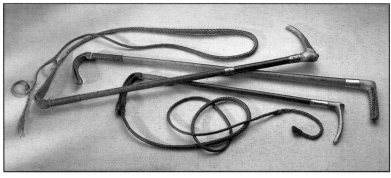

A selection of Victorian riding crops with
and without whip. These often carried the crest
or name of their owner.

PRICE GUIDE ❸

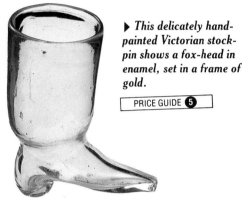

▶ This delicately hand-
painted Victorian stock-
pin shows a fox-head in
enamel, set in a frame of
gold.

PRICE GUIDE ❺

▲ Glass, silver and leather-
covered flasks, as well as bottles
shaped to fit their holders, were
carried for refreshment during
the hunt.

PRICE GUIDE ❺ ❻

▶ This glass stirrup cup takes
the unusual form of a riding boot
in contrast to the more
commonly found foxes' and
hounds' heads.

PRICE GUIDE ❹

with a quartern loaf on one side and a huge bologna
sausage on the other; besides these were nine eggs,
two pyramids of muffins and a great deal of toast,
while a dozen kidneys were spluttering on a spit
before the fire, and Betty held a gridiron covered
with mutton chops on the top . . .' Female guests
were usually ushered into a separate room, such as
the drawing room, where they were served sherry
and other refreshments. Only dedicated horse women
actually joined the hunt.

TALLY HO!

Breakfast over, the meet assembled with leading
hunt officers and followers wearing the distinguishing
scarlet coats, with the crested buttons of the hunt,
and a black velvet hat. The rest of the field wore
black or grey coats and top hats or bowlers. Most
riders wore dark waistcoats, white stocks, white
breeches and double-fold boots.

Once the stirrup cups had been passed, the
Master commanded the first draw (search) and the
hunting party rode out to the covert, unleashing 15 to
20 couples (pairs) of matched foxhounds. These
were controlled by the huntsman's voice and the
hunting horn, used to signal the sight of a fox.

At the end of a long day, most hunters were in
need of a strong refreshment. On arriving home,
many may well have taken a complete stirrup cup of
hot punch or a glass or two of whisky.

◀ The hounds are on to the scent and the hunt is in fully cry
– this very vigorous sport attracted only the bravest among
horsewomen.

The Life of a Working Dog

No Victorian country house was complete without its attendant
population of dogs, particularly guard dogs and gun dogs

A few of these dogs – the toy spaniels or
poodles, for instance – enjoyed a pampered
life indoors, but most other breeds slept in
kennels, working for their livings as gun
dogs, guard dogs or hunting hounds.
Among these, the setter was particularly
popular. Its intelligence and stamina made it
a capital companion for long days of
shooting over rough country. The pointer
and water spaniel were also admired for
their obedience and good nature (though one
Victorian guide acknowledged the dis-
advantage of the smell of a spaniel when
wet).

Greyhounds were kept only for hare
coursing and tended to be a bit snappish
with strangers. Foxhounds and beagles 'do
not belong in any sense to the household.'
warned *Cassell's Household Guide* in
1872, and these were kept in the hunt
kennels. There was a tradition, however,
called 'walking hound puppies' which consisted of various households taking a hound
puppy into their kennels for its first year, in
order to get it used to people and so that it
would behave properly at meets when
hunting.

Although the Victorians loved and
romanticized individual animals, cruel prac-
tices persisted. It was thought, for instance,
that burning the legs of a greyhound made it
swifter. As for the pointer, 'no variety is so
foully abused,' commented *Cassell's Household Guide*, which condemned the practice
of spraying an animal with small shot for a
mistake in the field.

▶▲ *Richard Andsell's painting entitled*
Watchful *and painted in 1848 depicts game
shooting on the moor.*

▶ *The majority of Victorian dogs had to work for
a living. Many were kept as shooting dogs,
trained to sniff out and retrieve game.*

▶ *No hunt could afford to neglect the welfare of a valuable pack. Often a special kennel hunstman was responsible for their care.*

▶▼ *Eugene Petit's mid-nineteenth century painting called* Duck Rising *shows English setters flushing wild duck on marshland.*

◀ *Although the Victorians could at times be hard on their animals, they loved to sentimentalize them in paintings. This work, called 'Waiting for Master' is typical of the period.*

◀◀ *Henri Schouten's painting, dated 1927 and entitled* Good Friends, *is a masterly portrait of working dogs keeping an alert eye while at rest.*

Taxidermy

The Victorians were avid collectors of stuffed wildlife.
Taxidermy, which was at its height then, fell out of fashion but
is once again proving popular

Eyes glazed and teeth bared, the head of a tiger stared down from the chimneybreast in the billiards room. Sprawled in front of the fire was a polar bear rug. Alongside the cue rack a cased pike, its jaws open, cast a glassy eye over the gentleman at the table.

In the 19th century, particularly the latter half, the craftsmanship of the taxidermist could be seen throughout the country house. And it was not confined to trophies of the hunting field. Much of the taxidermist's output was decorative and was admired by the ladies.

In the morning room a glass dome, known as a shade, enclosed a dozen hummingbirds whose iridescent wings caught the sun. A peacock, its bright train forever spread, was mounted as a pole screen in the drawing room to keep the heat of the flames from the ladies' faces. A silver-mounted hoof served as an inkstand on a writing table. And when the lady of the house dressed to pay a visit she wore a rabbit's foot brooch and white egret plumes in her hat – both prepared by the taxidermist.

THE COLLECTING SPIRIT
The Victorian period saw a marked upsurge of interest in nature. Birds' eggs, butterflies and plants from around the world were collected by scientists and keen amateurs. They also collected animal specimens. The Victorian naturalist worked on the principle that 'what's shot is history, what's missed is mystery.'

Eminent naturalists therefore built up enviable collections of British birds, adding rarities to them whenever the chance presented itself. A foreign bird making a landfall, for instance, on the Sussex coast would soon fall to a gun and later that day would be on the taxidermist's bench at Pratt & Sons of Brighton, to be mounted and sold on to a collector.

The enthusiasm for natural history, along with the exploits of hunters at home and abroad, kept taxidermists busy. Soon every town and many a village had one or more taxidermy firms.

HISTORY OF TAXIDERMY
William Swainson, the Victorian naturalist, defined taxidermy as 'the art of preserving animals bodies otherwise than in spirits'. By the 19th century this art had advanced to a point where animals could be preserved in a lifelike manner and would last for a considerable length of time.

Preservation of dead animals has a long history. The Egyptians embalmed cats and dogs to accompany their pharaohs. William

Shakespeare in *Romeo and Juliet* wrote:
'I do remember an apothecary . . .
And in his needy shop a tortoise hung,
An alligator stuff'd, and other skins
Of ill-shaped fishes . . .'

Taxidermy, as we recognize it, has probably been practised for less than 500 years. In 1516 a live rhino, being shipped as a gift from the King of Portugal to the Pope, drowned en route. To the Pope's great disappointment, it arrived at the Vatican stuffed. A 16th-century Dutch nobleman who kept tropical birds in a heated aviary lost them one night when they were asphyxiated by fumes from the heater. He had the corpses skinned, stuffed with spices and wired so that they could be mounted.

Spices were quite effective but by Victorian times a more usual preservative was arsenic. In a recipe laid down by Bécoeur, the 18th-century French taxidermist, arsenic was mixed with an equal quantity of white soap and smaller amounts

Animal Tableaux

WALTER POTTER WAS A VICTORIAN TAXIDERMIST WHO PRODUCED NUMEROUS INGENIOUS ANIMAL TABLEAUX. THIS ONE DEPICTS 'THE DEATH OF COCK ROBIN'. OTHERS SHOW ANIMALS IN HUMAN ROLES, WITH RED SQUIRRELS TAKING TEA OR RATS SQUABBLING OVER A GAME OF DOMINOES.

▲ *The naturalist who was unable to travel abroad could learn much from the study of stuffed foreign animals. The leading taxidermists often kept a photographic record of their best work. This book shows an enormous variety of heads and skins prepared by Gerards.*

The print is by the pioneer American naturalist, Audubon, who also practised taxidermy. Owls make very attractive mounted specimens – this is a tawny owl – and can be found in rectangular cases, domes or uncased.

around it are stuffed with tow or wood wool. Glass eyes replace the natural ones, wires support limbs or wings, while wax or plaster simulate the interior of the mouth. The skin is sewn up and supported in the desired position by thread and pieces of card for several weeks until it has dried.

The specimen is mounted on a baseboard or a branch, secured in place by the wires projecting through the feet. Groundwork – a representation of the animal's natural habitat – is then built up. Painted clay or papier-mâché are used to form rocks. Dried moss, wax leaves or plants preserved in glycerine are added. A painted backdrop might complete the scene. If it is too detailed it may detract from the specimen – an evocative watercolour is most effective.

A VICTORIAN PASSION

Taxidermy received a real boost from the Great Exhibition of 1851. John Gould, taxidermist to the Zoological Society and publisher of several natural history books, exhibited cases containing 1,500 stuffed hummingbirds. Displayed at Regent's Park Zoo, these proved one of the great attractions of 1851, drawing 75,000 visitors including Queen Victoria. At later exhibitions, Rowland Ward produced dramatic large tableaux showing red deer stags fighting and tigers attacking an elephant in the Indian jungle.

The vogue for taxidermy was established and no Victorian country house would be complete without its trophy heads mounted on the walls and a dome of exotic birds or charming red squirrels to delight the ladies.

▼ *Owners of country houses often built up large collections, generally by one taxidermist. These are at Calke Abbey, Derbyshire.*

of camphor, salt of tartar and lime to form a preservative known as arsenical soap. This not only preserved the skin and prevented the decay of any remaining flesh but was also thought to be effective against insect attack.

Various eminent taxidermists nevertheless opted for safer preservatives. Charles Waterton swore by corrosive sublimate, while Rowland Ward and Montagu Browne developed their own patent formulas. Borax, which is non-toxic, is the most widely used preservative today.

TECHNIQUES

The processes of cleaning, stuffing and mounting developed in the 19th century are broadly the same today. For birds and mammals a cut is made in the skin, allowing the skin to be peeled back and the flesh scraped away. The bones are removed, leaving only the skull, and the skin is treated with preservative. A body of wadding or a framework of wires is inserted and the gaps

Fish and Birds

The London firm of J. Cooper & Sons, which finally closed its doors in the 1950s, was the leading specialist in fish taxidermy for around 100 years. Many of the cases found today will have been preserved by Cooper's. Stuffing a fish was more time consuming than other forms of taxidermy and many taxidermists avoided this work. The skin lost its colour on death and therefore had to be painted (ideally scale by scale) to restore a natural look, and was lightly varnished to give it a gloss.

Some stuffed fish actually contain no part of the original specimen, as they are plaster casts or wooden carvings. If they are well executed they can be as collectable as genuine specimens. Many fish are mounted in bow-fronted glass cases with interior gilt lettering detailing the fish's particulars – this adds to the attraction. Until the 1930s Cooper's cases had a pale blue background; later cases have a pale green one. All have a setting of underwater plants. Some include the line and hook on which the fish was taken.

Birds were the stock in trade of all taxidermists. Cases produced for the parlour often had birds from around the world, all clustered in one bush. Today's collector usually prefers a naturalistic setting with a single bird or a pair in a good case. Cases prepared by Gunn's of Norwich were well executed and have generally survived in good condition. Those by James Gardner of London have, however, often been affected by beetles and moths. Cases by Murray of Carnforth, Hine of Southport and Peter Spicer of Leamington often contain an attractive painted backdrop.

◀ A case of doves by an unknown taxidermist. These domesticated or town birds are an unusual subject. The composition is a little awkward but the groundwork of rocks and grasses is good.

PRICE GUIDE 5

▼ The odd juxtaposition of species that would never naturally be found together somewhat detracts from the good groundwork. Perched in the branches are a jay, bullfinches, hawfinches and a goldcrest between the carrion crow and the curlew.

PRICE GUIDE 5

PRICE GUIDE

Caught by S. TURPIN, at Marlow, Nov. 6th 1928. Wgt. 13½lbs.

▼ *A roach by Cooper's. Mounted in 1943, it has the green background of later cases with the gilt edging and lettering typical of the firm.*

PRICE GUIDE **6**

▲ *A stuffed pike by Cooper's. The blue background is typical of their early cases and the bow-fronted glass was another hallmark. Cooper's label can just be seen at the top right.*

PRICE GUIDE **7**

ROACH 2 lbs ¼ oz
Caught at Fordingbridge by C. Newman 26th Feb 1943

▼ *Cooper's sometimes mounted birds. This peregrine by them was taken on the Isle of Mull and auctioned in 1893.*

PRICE GUIDE **7**

◄ *A typical Victorian dome of exotic birds mounted on a lichened twig with dry grasses. Species here include orioles, honey-eaters, cardinals and tanagers.*

PRICE GUIDE **5**

PRICE GUIDE

▲ An unusual piece of Wardian furniture – candlesticks made of porcupine quills.

PRICE GUIDE ④

▲ An ashtray mounted on a bison's hoof, and a matchbox holder on an antelope's hoof.

PRICE GUIDE ④

▲ An elephant's foot liqueur case holding four decanters. Dating from around 1900, it was prepared by Gerards.

PRICE GUIDE ⑥

▲ An otter mask mounted by Peter Spicer of Leamington for the Tetcott Otter Hounds. The animal was caught at Bude on August 31st, 1925.

PRICE GUIDE ⑤

▲ A Victorian sporting trophy. This head of a white-eared cob is in relatively good condition for its age, though the ears are a bit ragged.

PRICE GUIDE ⑤

PRICE GUIDE

Mammals

Stuffed mammals can be collected in three different forms. Firstly, there are the trophy heads where the head (sometimes including the neck) is mounted on a wooden shield, often with its details on a metal plaque. These, along with horns similarly mounted, are designed to be hung on the wall.

Secondly, and perhaps most attractive, are complete stuffed mammals which may be cased or uncased. Cased specimens (smaller species may be in a dome) usually have appropriate groundwork.

Thirdly, there is Wardian furniture – items made from a part of an animal. This somewhat unusual area includes elephant's foot wastepaper baskets, fox paw paper knives and pincushions made from hooves.

British species are generally cheaper than exotic animals from abroad. Something such as a hippo's head is hard to come by, expensive and likely to be in poor condition due to its age.

The firm of Rowland Ward of London produced a good deal of Wardian furniture but was best known for its trophy heads. Hibbs of Ollerton, Murray of Carnforth, Peter Spicer of Leamington and the Shaws of Shrewsbury were also noted for their trophy heads.

Good complete mammals, usually cased, were prepared by Peter Spicer, the Shaws and by Hutchings of Aberystwyth. The hallmark of Hutchings' foxes is the item of prey which was invariably included. This was generally a grey partridge.

◄ *A female brassos monkey. Good quality foreign specimens such as this rarely come on to the market. Zoos provide a very limited source of new specimens.*

PRICE GUIDE ❻

▲ *A fox mask mounted by Peter Spicer of Leamington. The taxidermist's name is stamped on the back of the wooden shield. The metal plaque indicates that the fox was caught by the South Tetcott Foxhounds on August 23rd, 1921. As one would expect with a piece by Spicer, the head is well mounted and in fair condition.*

PRICE GUIDE ❺

◄ *An impala head mounted by an unknown taxidermist earlier this century. The shield provides no information except the country of origin – Tanganyika. It looks as though it has been stroked too often and is rather threadbare. Moths may be responsible for the tattered ears.*

PRICE GUIDE ❺

PRICE GUIDE

COLLECTOR'S TIPS

Poor Taxidermy

AN AWFUL OTTER. HEAD AND LEGS ARE ANATOMICALLY WRONG, POSTURE IS WRONG AND THE REEDS ARE SHORT.

Twenty years ago it was possible to buy a stuffed cased salmon for less than the price of a fresh one. Stuffed birds and mammals could be picked up for a few pounds in junk shops. Taxidermy was out of fashion and had been so since the inter-war years. The past ten years or so have seen a revival of interest and prices reflect this.

It is worth remembering that freshly stuffed specimens by today's taxidermists will cost about the same as those from the turn of the century. Quite a few amateurs dabble in taxidermy and their work is of variable quality. It is best to buy from an experienced, qualified craftsman, preferably one who is museum trained. The specimen's colours will be fresh and his work will last for many years.

Today's wildlife protection laws are stringent and few species can be freely taken. Pest species and, in season, game species are readily available but most other wildlife will rarely come on to the market unless a newly dead specimen that has died from natural causes or met with an accident finds its way into a taxidermist's hands. The only practical way to collect rarer species — those such as golden eagle, snowy owl and otter — is to buy old specimens.

Taxidermists and dealers must be government licensed, whether they are selling old or new specimens, so it is rare to find taxidermy in general antique shops. Country house auctions can be another source of old specimens.

Although many cases are not labelled, the leading practitioners often marked their

Cased Birds by Spicer

A PAIR OF RED GROUSE BY PETER SPICER OF LEAMINGTON. THIS IS A GOOD CASE BUT IT SHOULD BE REMEMBERED THAT EVEN THE BEST TAXIDERMY FIRMS PRODUCED SOME POOR WORK DURING THE MANY DECADES THEY WERE IN BUSINESS.

THE PAINTED BACKDROP TONES IN WELL WITH THE BIRDS AND SUBTLY EVOKES THEIR MOUNTAIN AND MOORLAND HABITAT WITHOUT BEING OVERPOWERING. THE GROUNDWORK OF ROCKS, LICHEN AND HEATHER COMPLETES THE PICTURE.

THE BIRDS ARE WELL COMPOSED AND HAVE KEPT THEIR NATURAL COLOUR (AS HAS THE HEATHER). THEIR PLUMAGE IS IN GOOD CONDITION AND SHOWS NO SIGN OF DAMAGE BY INSECTS. THE COCK BIRD IS ON THE LEFT.

THE CASE IS TYPICAL OF SPICER, WITH THREE GLASS SIDES, GOLD BEADING AND BLACK PAINTED WOOD.

① A WATERCOLOUR BACKDROP WHICH COMPLEMENTS THE BIRDS

② WELL MOUNTED BIRDS IN A TYPICALLY ALERT POSITION

③ GROUNDWORK OF ROCKS AND LICHEN CONJURE UP THE BIRDS' HABITAT

④ A SIGNED PEBBLE AMONG THE GROUNDWORK WAS SPICER'S HALLMARK

⑤ A CLASSICALLY SIMPLE CASE, TYPICAL OF PETER SPICER

·CLOSE·UP·

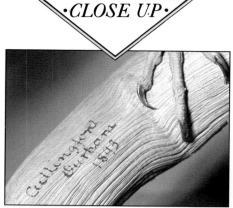

① **TAXIDERMIST'S SIGNATURE**

① A SIGNATURE ON A BRANCH OF MERLINS PREPARED FOR LEICESTER MUSEUM BY CULLINGFORD OF DURHAM IN 1893.

② A TIGER'S HEAD (PART OF A RUG) BY ROWLAND WARD. THE TONGUE, GUMS AND ROOF OF THE MOUTH HAVE BEEN WELL MODELLED.

③ A HEAD IN GOOD CONDITION FOR A VICTORIAN PIECE BUT FEATHERS HAVE COME LOOSE NEAR THE BILL — PERHAPS DUE TO INSECTS.

④ PETER SPICER'S STAMP ON THE BACK OF A WOODEN SHIELD ON WHICH A HEAD IS MOUNTED.

⑤ MURRAY'S LABEL FROM THE BACK OF A CASE ACTS AS AN ADVERTISEMENT FOR HIS SERVICES.

⑥ A DISC SET NEATLY INTO THE GROUNDWORK OF A CASE IDENTIFIES ROWLAND WARD'S WORK.

② **TIGER'S MOUTH**

③ **JAY'S HEAD**

④ **TAXIDERMIST'S STAMP**

⑤ **TAXIDERMIST'S LABEL**

⑥ **ROWLAND WARD'S DISC LABEL**

work in some way. Generally this took the form of a printed label on the back of a case. Sometimes there is a signature on the inside of a case upright or on a branch. Peter Spicer included a signed pebble with his groundwork. The taxidermist's name may be included in the inscription on a fish case. An experienced specialist dealer can identify the work of many taxidermists by their style and the design of the case itself.

WHAT TO LOOK FOR

When buying a work, personal preference is the main criterion. A rabbit in a pleasing case with good groundwork may be more attractive than an uncased, glowering falcon. Collectors can be eclectic or they may specialize in areas such as fish, ducks or British mammals. Stag's heads and similar trophies are often too big for today's homes as they need a large, high room to be displayed to effect. Smaller fox masks (mounted heads) may be more suitable.

Groundwork and backdrops are usually self-evidently good or bad. However, unless you are familiar with animals in the wild, it can be harder to determine whether a pose is lifelike or not. Take along a friend who knows the subject or rely on the dealer.

POINTS TO WATCH

■ Specimens exposed to sunlight will have faded, losing much of their natural colour. Avoid these.

■ Insect damage can affect cased and uncased specimens. Fur or feathers will look ragged. Check especially the area around the eye. Fish are less prone to damage.

■ Uncased specimens may have been dulled and darkened by accumulated dirt. They can be cleaned by an expert but it is not cheap.

■ Fake maker's labels — usually crude photocopies — have been attached to the work of lesser taxidermists. Unless you are familiar with the taxidermist's style, buy only from a reputable dealer.

▲ *A turtle's head is an unusual piece. This one was caught near Hong Kong in 1916.*

Swords and Daggers

Nineteenth century swords and daggers were not only functional but beautiful. British and foreign examples provide an insight into military life in the far-flung outposts of the Empire

By the last quarter of the 19th century, the British Empire had become an Aladdin's cave for many of its administrators and soldiers, most of whom came from families which had never travelled abroad before. Naturally they returned with souvenirs and the most appropriate souvenir for a soldier was, of course, his adversary's sword or dagger.

Curios of this kind were not always exhibited with pride. Often they were put to practical use, as amusing paper-knives or even for cutting tobacco. Larger collections might be displayed in glass-topped cases, but usually daggers and swords were hung on the wall, whenever possible in crossed pairs with naked blades in imitation of the Scottish broadswords of baronial halls.

The countless variations you find in the grip and hand-guard on the hilt cannot disguise the fact that the sword-blade has

COMPARISONS

Indian Weapons

EUROPEAN SWORDS WERE OFTEN EXTREMELY DECORATIVE BUT FEW COULD RIVAL THE SPLENDOUR DISPLAYED BY THIS JEWELLED-HILTED INDIAN SWORD BROUGHT BACK BY CLIVE OF INDIA AS A PRIZE FROM HIS CAMPAIGNS DURING THE 18TH CENTURY.

changed remarkably little since the Iron Age and not that much since the first edged weapons were cast in copper and bronze.

DESIGNED FOR COMBAT

Essentially, there are only three things you can do with a sword: cut, thrust and parry. Changing fashions in warfare and armour have meant that at times cutting weapons have been more effective, at others thrusting ones like the short, stabbing swords of the Greeks and Romans, which suited disciplined armies fighting in formation. In con-

trast, the huge double-edge broadswords of the Vikings and Crusaders were designed for a more individualistic style of combat.

It was in Renaissance Italy and Spain that swordsmanship became a truly scientific skill. The weapon used by soldier and civilian alike was the long sharp-pointed rapier with its guard of intricately entwined bars. These rapiers of the 16th and 17th century are the first European swords that qualify as beautiful antiques rather than rusty archaeological artefacts and the finest are rare museum pieces. Less well-

▶ *Treasured swords decorate the walls of this room in which a fencing match is taking place. This sport is practised with special weapons and demonstrates skill in swordsmanship.*

▼ *The traditional way of hanging swords is bare-bladed and crossed, as if to emulate their use in battle. Some were never used in combat but were made simply as dress swords.*

preserved ones do still come on the market, however. Equally attractive are the small-swords carried by the 18th century gentleman, although these were rarely used, being little more than ornaments worn to set off a shapely calf.

DECLINE OF THE SWORD

By Victorian times, apart from serving officers, only courtiers and diplomats continued to wear swords as part of their daily dress. The sword was fast disappearing from the battlefield, too. Throughout the 19th century, it was only the cavalry who regularly used swords on active service. Modern warfare required a curved weapon that could deliver a slashing cut in the manner of a Turkish *janizary* with a point rigid enough for a fatal thrust. Somehow, despite the miracles of scientific progress, the cavalry troopers' swords were never satisfactory and complaints about the various designs came back from every foreign campaign: in the Crimea the swords could not pierce a Russian greatcoat, in the Sudan they simply bent. Blades were imported from Solingen in the North Rhineland, a small town which for centuries had produced swords reckoned to be the finest in Europe, but results were no better. Not until 1908 did they come up with a 'perfect' design, too late for it to be put to the test.

Among the other services which were issued with swords during the 19th century were the Navy, the Pioneer Corps and even the Police, but these had to make do with cheap workaday weapons. The most spectacular swords still in use were those carried by officers of the Highland Regiments with their traditional basket-hilts lined with buckskin or other soft leather. Another unusual weapon still carried today by Scottish officers is the dirk, made originally from a cut-down sword blade with a decorative carved ebony hilt.

THE VICTORIAN CHOICE

The Victorian collector cared little for British weapons, unless they had some historical significance attached to them, as, for example, broadswords and dirks of the Jacobite rebellions. Military families would naturally have their personal collections, in which pride of place went to swords presented on the occasion of great victories, or those surrendered by a defeated foe. Individual regiments amassed similar tangi-

ble chronicles of their own history. Of other collectors, some were true swordsmen, who cherished a piece for its effectiveness, rather than for its history or beauty. Then there were sporting gentlemen who collected hunting swords, short weapons like long daggers with a grip of ivory or horn and little or no guard. The most assiduous collectors, however, were inspired not just by antiquity and fine workmanship, but by anthropological curiosity.

SAMURAI SWORDS

It was during the second half of the 19th century that Europeans became aware that there still existed a culture where the sword was held in greater veneration than it ever had been in the Christian or Islamic world. This, of course, was Japan, where, until a decree of 1876, Samurai still went about their daily business armed with the two swords symbolic to their class. At first, Westerners were simply dazzled by the intricate craftsmanship of the decorative sword-furniture. They were even more amazed when they learnt that all the great families of swordsmiths were known by name and that each one could be recognized by an expert from the pattern produced by the fusion of iron and steel on the blade.

In Japan, the loss of one's sword was equated with the loss of one's soul, an attitude which persisted right up to the Second World War and is still found in conservative Japanese today. Imagine the horror and shame a Japanese soldier would have felt to see auction rooms selling off lots in which swords were bundled up with fencing foils, walking sticks and even golf-clubs. This was a common occurrence in the 1950s, but since then the enthusiasm of collectors and dealers has ensured that swords are treated once more with the reverence they deserve.

British Military Swords

Today's collector can still find a good number of 18th century weapons, but at that time regiments followed no set pattern in how they chose to arm themselves. Since then there have been a series of regulations laying down what kind of sword each rank should carry on every occasion, which makes identification a much simpler task.

Although 19th century officers' swords were supposed to be of standard design, there were slight variations, because the officer usually ordered his sword either from his tailor or from a sword-cutler. The latter was not a manufacturer; he merely assembled blades and hilts ordered from elsewhere. In 1822 infantry officers were prescribed the 'Gothic' hilt, a lattice of gilt bars, while light cavalry officers' hilts of the same period were simpler three-barred affairs. As time went by, most hilts were simplified into a scroll of decorated sheet steel incorporating the regimental badge or monogram.

Such soulless utilitarianism was not the order of the day throughout the entire army. The Highland Regiments kept their patriotic broadswords and dirks, and generals and staff officers carried weapons worthy of their splendid uniforms. Generals' swords are obviously few and far between, but almost as impressive are the levée swords of cavalry officers. These are in the same scimitar-shaped 'mameluke' style adopted for a time by British generals in imitation of Napoleon's commanders.

A succession of different designs were produced for use by the British forces and these are known as 'patterns' specified by their date of first issue.

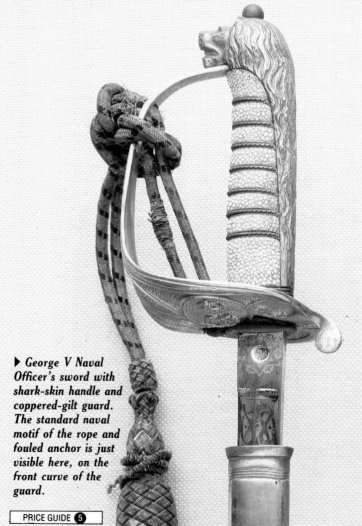

▶ George V Naval Officer's sword with shark-skin handle and coppered-gilt guard. The standard naval motif of the rope and fouled anchor is just visible here, on the front curve of the guard.

PRICE GUIDE **5**

▶ The style of this Light Cavalry sabre, dated 1830-40, is known as the 1796 pattern. It has a characteristic, P-shaped knuckle-bow. This one also has a pipe-backed blade and steel scabbard.

PRICE GUIDE **5**

PRICE GUIDE

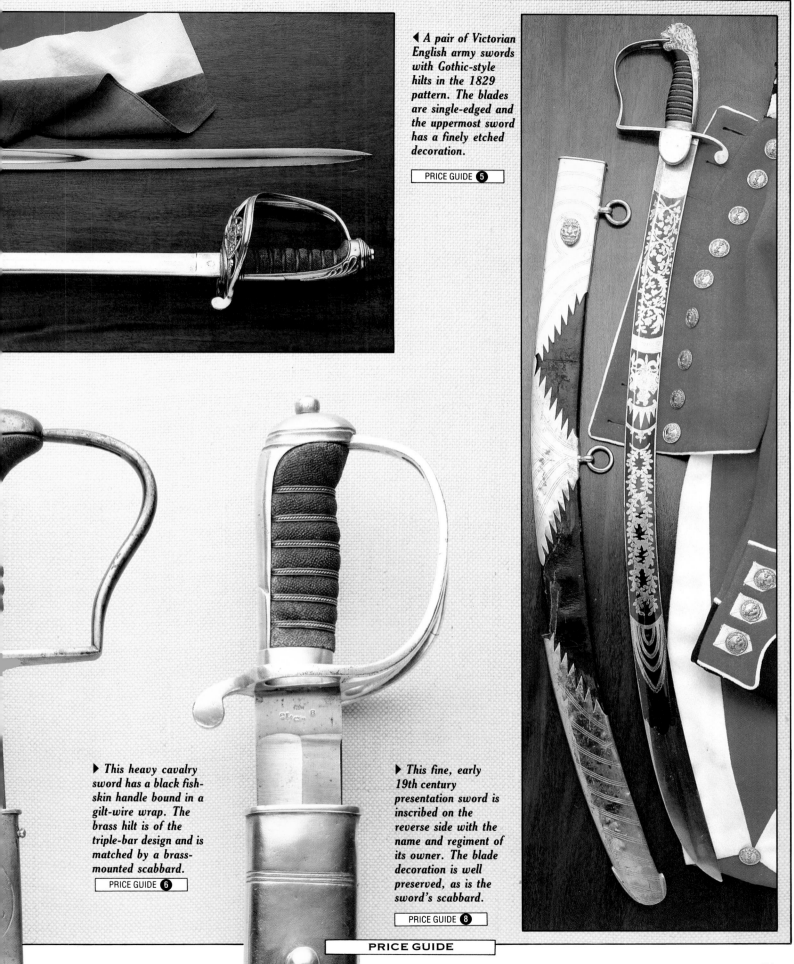

◀ *A pair of Victorian English army swords with Gothic-style hilts in the 1829 pattern. The blades are single-edged and the uppermost sword has a finely etched decoration.*

PRICE GUIDE **5**

▶ *This heavy cavalry sword has a black fish-skin handle bound in a gilt-wire wrap. The brass hilt is of the triple-bar design and is matched by a brass-mounted scabbard.*

PRICE GUIDE **6**

▶ *This fine, early 19th century presentation sword is inscribed on the reverse side with the name and regiment of its owner. The blade decoration is well preserved, as is the sword's scabbard.*

PRICE GUIDE **8**

PRICE GUIDE

Foreign Swords and Daggers

Given the time and the money, the swords everyone would like to collect are Japanese ones. However, since the history and lore of Japanese swords require a lifetime's study, not forgetting that you must learn Japanese to decipher the swordsmith's inscriptions, you would have to put your trust in the opinions of the experts.

Slightly less daunting are the swords and daggers of the Islamic world. Although this stretches from North Africa to Indonesia, it has long been familiar territory to the British soldier and many fine pieces found their way back to this country in the 19th century. Persian blades in particular are famous for their 'watered' steel. This beautiful effect is in fact achieved by the use of acids to emphasize the impurities in the steel. Many Middle-eastern blades can also be 'damascened' – that is, decorated with gold or silver laid onto the steel. Each country had its typical weapons – Turkey the *yataghan* and the *shamshir*, Persia the single-edged dagger called a *kard* and Arabia the short, ferociously curved *jambiya* – although the manufacture of these types spread across Asia as far as India.

India itself boasts a bewildering variety of weapons, the most characteristic being the *talwar*, with its disc pommel-shaped like a teapot lid. If it is oddities you are in search of, traditional Sri Lankan swords have hilts in the shape of dragons' heads, the wavy-bladed *kris* and *sundang* from Malaya and Indonesia might appeal, or you could even favour the misshapen *kukri* of the Ghurkas.

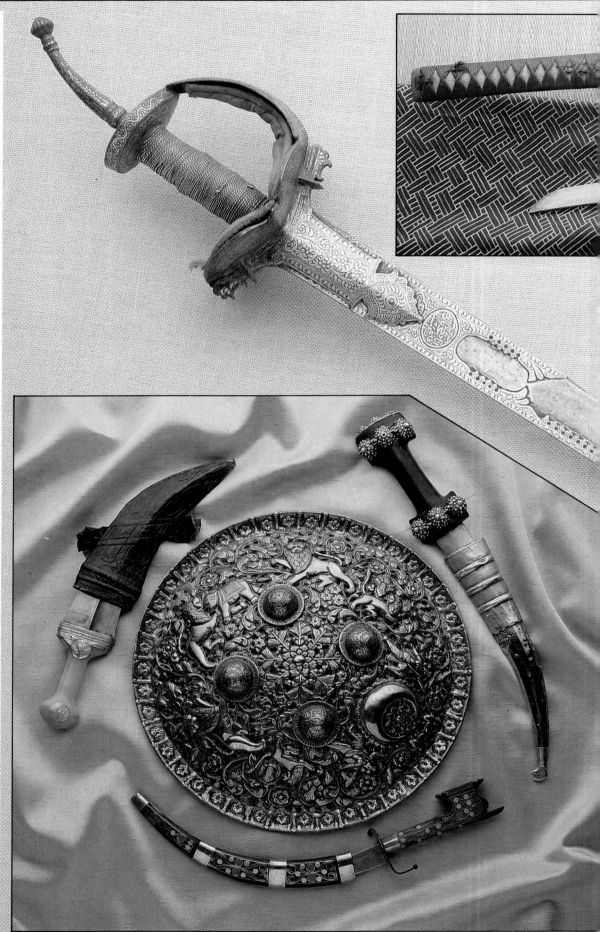

PRICE GUIDE

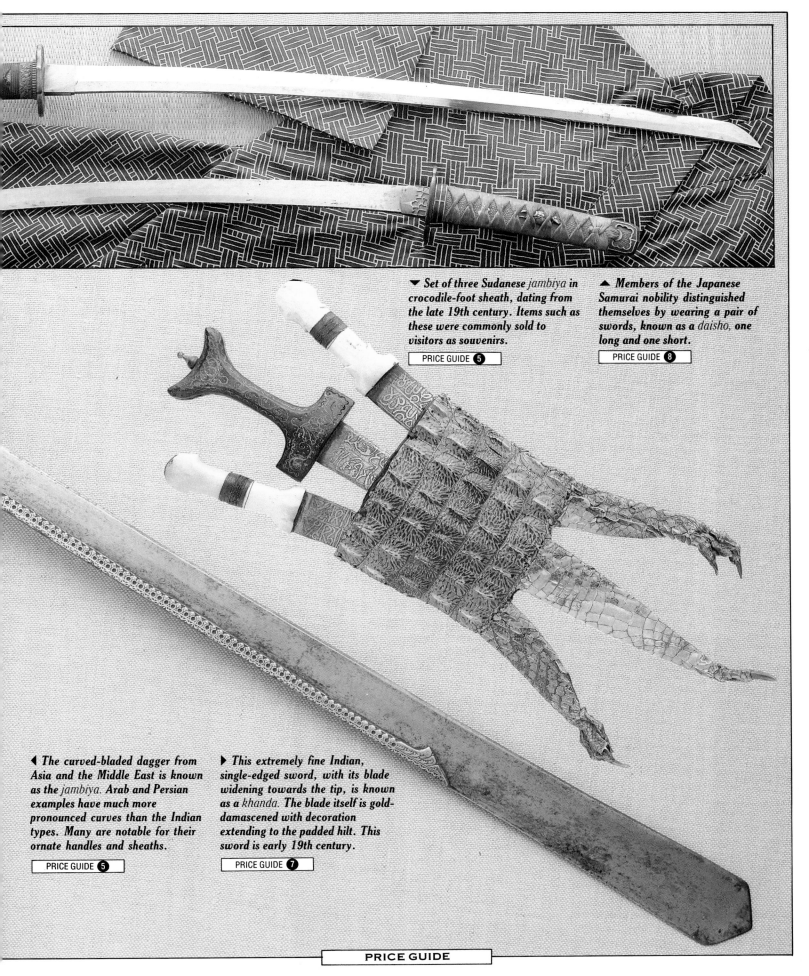

▼ Set of three Sudanese *jambiya* in crocodile-foot sheath, dating from the late 19th century. Items such as these were commonly sold to visitors as souvenirs.

PRICE GUIDE **5**

▲ Members of the Japanese Samurai nobility distinguished themselves by wearing a pair of swords, known as a *daisho*, one long and one short.

PRICE GUIDE **8**

◀ The curved-bladed dagger from Asia and the Middle East is known as the *jambiya*. Arab and Persian examples have much more pronounced curves than the Indian types. Many are notable for their ornate handles and sheaths.

PRICE GUIDE **5**

▶ This extremely fine Indian, single-edged sword, with its blade widening towards the tip, is known as a *khanda*. The blade itself is gold-damascened with decoration extending to the padded hilt. This sword is early 19th century.

PRICE GUIDE **7**

PRICE GUIDE

COLLECTOR'S TIPS

When a Japanese expert judges a sword, he does so by its feel and balance as much as by its appearance. The sword has a character all its own, and it is not easy for the beginner to understand what is right or appropriate when looking at a sword.

Only when you have handled a number of weapons can you have any idea of what constitutes a good sword or be really sure what appeals to you.

With so many of the finest pieces in museums or permanent collections, the beginner is obviously limited by what is available.

If you decide to collect British (or European) military swords, the business of recognition will be considerably easier than it is with other collectors' items, for the simple reason that armies like their equipment to be clearly marked. It is very rare to find a 19th century sword with no information on it at all; there is almost always something engraved or stamped on the blade or the hilt. The information may be misleading: the running wolf mark of Solingen and the name J. J. Runkel often appear on British swords, the maker's number may be confused with a date, and the name and date on the sword may not have been engraved by the first owner (in which case you are in luck). If it has nothing else, an officer's sword should at least carry the royal cypher, though in the case of Queen Victoria this is not a great help in dating the sword exactly.

RECOGNIZING FAKES

Reference books are an essential aid in identifying and dating military swords, but they cannot cover every example you encounter. Some pieces refuse to fit the pattern; the hilt and blade do not belong together. Usually there is no need to suspect

Real or Fake?

WITH THE CONTINUING DEMAND FOR ORNAMENTAL *JAMBIYA*, REPRODUCTIONS CONTINUE TO BE PRODUCED. IT WOULD BE EASY TO CONFUSE THE GENUINE ARTICLE FROM 19TH CENTURY MOROCCO (LEFT) WITH THIS VERY SIMILAR RECENT REPRO.

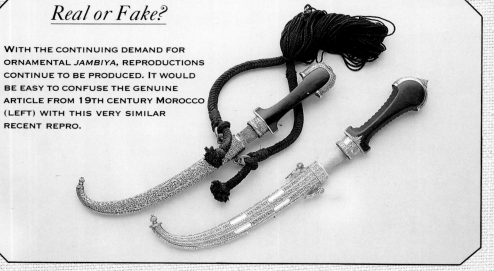

British Officer's Sword

BRITISH FIGHTING SWORDS OF THE 19TH CENTURY WERE DESCENDED FROM THE EARLIER, HEAVY, CUT-AND-THRUST TYPE. THEY WERE MAINLY WORN BY MOUNTED ARMY OFFICERS, AND ALSO NAVAL OFFICERS, WHILE THE LOWER RANKS CARRIED SMALLER WEAPONS. THE VARIOUS PATTERNS THAT WERE ISSUED CONTINUED TO EVOLVE THROUGHOUT THE CENTURY WITH SIMILAR SWORDS WORN BY THE VARIOUS REGIMENTS, BUT DIFFERENTIATED BY GRIP MATERIAL, HILT-STYLE AND PARTICULAR REGIMENTAL BADGE.

THIS SWORD, DATED AT AROUND 1855, BELONGED TO AN OFFICER IN THE BRITISH RIFLE BRIGADE. IT IS IMMEDIATELY RECOGNIZABLE AS AN ARMY SWORD, AS NAVAL SWORDS TENDED TO HAVE A CLOSED HAND-GUARD RATHER THAN THE OPEN-LATTICED TYPE DISPLAYED HERE.

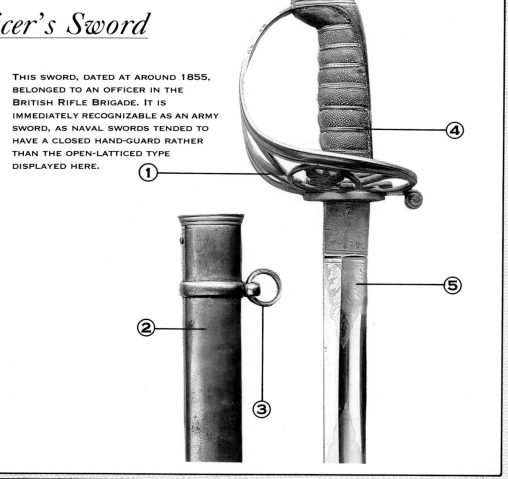

① GOTHIC-STYLE HILT, SO-CALLED BECAUSE OF THE POINTED ARCHES FORMING THE DESIGN.

② STEEL SCABBARD MATCHES STEEL HILT AND IS SHAPED TO FIT THE SWORD SNUGLY.

③ TWO BANDS AND RINGS FOR SUSPENSION WERE STANDARD ON THE SCABBARD.

④ BLACK FISH-SKIN GRIP WITH STEEL BACK-PIECE TERMINATING IN CAP POMMEL.

⑤ SHARP, STEEL BLADE BEARS FINELY-ETCHED DECORATION.

·CLOSE UP·

① **ROYAL CYPHER**

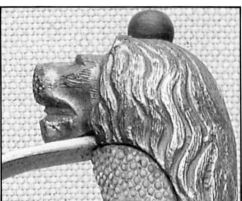

② **HINGED GUARD**

① THE ROYAL CYPHER APPEARED ON ENGLISH ARMY SWORDS. HERE, 'VR' DENOTES VICTORIA'S REIGN.

② THE GUARD ON THIS BRITISH SWORD IS NEATLY HINGED TO MAKE IT COMFORTABLE TO WEAR.

③ A LION'S HEAD TERMINAL ON THE POMMEL WAS EXTREMELY COMMON ON EUROPEAN SWORDS.

④ A PRESENTATION INSCRIPTION ADDS GREATLY TO THE INTEREST AND VALUE OF A SWORD.

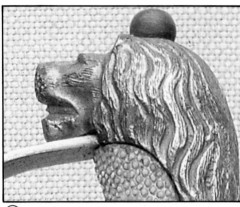

③ **LION-HEAD POMMEL**

TO MAJOR JAMES HOPE
SEC^nd BATT^n 2nd REG^t ROYAL EDINBURGH
VOLUNTEERS FROM THE OFFICERS
OF THAT BATTALION.

④ **PRESENTATION INSCRIPTION**

WRITTEN MARKINGS

THE SWORD CUTLER'S NAME APPEARED ON EUROPEAN SWORDS AS AN IMPRESSED MARK ON THE BLADE (BOTTOM). THE SCRIPT APPEARING ON THIS INDIAN SWORD (TOP) IS, HOWEVER, A PRAYER TO GOD.

skulduggery: the original purchaser may have had the sword made up to his own requirements or, more probably, the anomaly is simply the result of use.

WEAR AND TEAR

A sword used in earnest was not expected to last for ever. Owners often fitted new blades or grips and occasionally a whole new hilt. Fakes do exist, of course, but they are usually of older swords like rapiers, which turn up with hilts that have been cast in a mould. It is not difficult to distinguish between these and the lovingly hammered and chiselled originals. Rather than the sword or part of it being a fake, the deception may lie in an inscription linking it with some famous name or battle. Pay for the sword itself, not a spurious legend.

POINTS TO WATCH

■ Look for a suspiciously new hilt.
■ Check that the blade is appropriate for the style of hilt.
■ Hilt and blade should fit together perfectly; otherwise, suspect a marriage.
■ Does the blade feel too heavy or too light?
■ Check that the scabbard is of the same age as the sword. An original scabbard, however battered, increases the value.
■ Look for signs of wear and tear; cracks, rust, scratches and missing bars on the hilt. Be certain you know exactly what you are paying for.

▶ *This rather gruesome Pioneer's sword, with its serrated top edge, was used by English and German soldiers for chopping wood.*

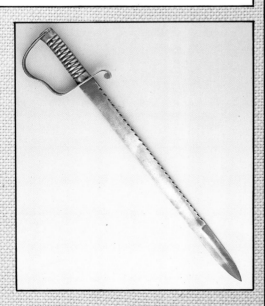

Colt Revolvers and Rifles

Revolvers and rifles played an important part in mid 19th century America, with Samuel Colt's name central to the history of such weapons

Samuel Colt was born in 1814 in Hartford, Connecticut, and from an early age he had a fascination for firearms. As a youth he joined the merchant navy and while at sea he occupied his mind playing around with a new idea – a revolver that could fire six times without reloading. Colt whittled his early designs out of wood and his crude carvings helped him to develop a revolver which was to become famous throughout the world.

THE FIRST REVOLVERS

Colt engaged the services of an American gunmaker called John Pearson in Baltimore who produced the first prototype revolving weapons to Samuel Colt's ideas. The general specification of these early models was a single rifled barrel which was aligned with a cylinder bored with six holes to hold a quantity of black powder and six lead bullets loaded from the front – hence the term muzzle-loading. The barrel and cylinder were held in a frame that had a pistol grip and spurred hammer that was cocked by the thumb for each individual shot. This system is called single action as opposed to double action which is commonplace today. The trigger folded away and was easily flicked out by the forefinger.

The revolver was fired by fitting a copper cap containing a fulminate of mercury over the protrusion called a nipple, screwed into the back of each of the six cavities in the cylinder. When the hammer struck the copper caps they would explode, sending sparks down the small hole bored into each nipple. These would then instantaneously ignite the black powder, transforming it into gas which, because it was trapped inside a metal cylinder, built up pressure and forced the lead bullet through the barrel of the weapon at great speed. The rifle barrel spun the bullet giving the projectile a centrifugal force which heightened its accuracy. On re-cocking the weapon in order to fire further shots, the hammer was pulled back and the internal mechanism revolved the cylinder (hence the term revolver) to the next loaded chamber. Thus Samuel Colt's revolver could be fired as quickly as a man could cock the gun and pull the trigger.

Due to a design fault the first gun fired all the chambers off together and the gun blew up, but Colt and Pearson persevered and produced a small group of rifles and revolvers that were the foundation of the first practical revolving firearms.

COLT PATERSONS

In 1835 Samuel Colt visited France and England taking out patents on his invention and he formed the Patent Arms Manufacturing Company at Paterson, New Jersey, which produced a total of about 2000 Colt revolving arms. All were muzzle-loading, percussion weapons: the rammed down gunpowder and lead bullet in each chamber were fired when a small percussion-cap was struck by the hammer of the weapon. Single-action revolvers predominated, although rifles, shotguns and carbines (short

The Early Rifle

MADE AROUND 1630, THIS IS A FINE EXAMPLE OF A WHEEL-LOCK RIFLE WITH ITS ATTRACTIVE BONE AND IVORY INLAY. THE TERM 'WHEEL-LOCK' REFERS TO THE LOCK WHICH WAS USED FOR FIRING THE RIFLE BY MEANS OF A SMALL STEEL WHEEL. LATER IN THE 17TH CENTURY THE WHEEL-LOCK GAVE WAY TO THE FLINT-LOCK, WHICH WAS LESS CUMBERSOME IN OPERATION.

rifles originally used by the cavalry), some self-cocking, were also made. These early products are referred to by collectors today as Colt Patersons and are extremely rare and valuable. In 1842 the Paterson company failed and Colt recovered little more than his US patent rights for the venture.

With the start of the American war with Mexico four years later, in 1846, there was

▼ *A cased Colt pocket revolver. Among the items included with the gun are an oil bottle, bullet mould, powder flask, caps and bullets. On the trade label inside the box are full instructions for loading and cleaning the gun.*

▲ *Samuel Colt's name is familiar to anyone with more than a passing interest in firearms. He patented his own unique system, the Colt revolving mechanism, which revolutionized the gun industry.*

an upsurge in demand for weapons and in particular for revolvers with the repeating action. As the original Paterson design had various faults, an improved model was made which was a single-action percussion revolver, six-chambered .44 calibre and with a 9 in (23 cm) barrel. (The calibre refers to the size of the bullet or the internal diameter of the barrel, and is expressed as a percentage of an inch.) Known to modern collectors as the Walker, Whitneyville-Walker or Model 1847 revolver, this weapon differed from its predecessors by using fewer lock-mechanism components, a trigger-guard and a powerful, hinged loading lever or rammer.

FAILURE IN ENGLAND

By 1847 Colt had his own factory in Hartford, Connecticut, which is still in production today. He also opened a factory at Bessborough Place in London which was in operation from January 1853 until December 1856. The short life of the factory has been blamed on the British gun trade, bad labour relations and the British Army's adoption of a competing revolver.

Colt Revolvers

Since Colt produced so many revolvers, it is best to narrow the field down to the best known models.

After the Paterson and Walker models came the Dragoon, a six-shot single-action .44 calibre percussion revolver, manufactured from 1848 to 1860 and the Navy, a six-shot single-action percussion revolver of .36 calibre. About 215,000 of these guns were made between 1851 and 1860. Another six-shot single-action .44 calibre percussion revolver known as the Army was made from 1860 until 1872 and, from 1873 until 1941, the Frontier was manufactured. Known as SAA – Single-Action Army – it was a six-shot single-action revolver and was made in various calibres. The Peacemaker was identical to the Frontier model except that it was chambered for .45 calibre cartridges and weighed slightly less.

▶ *A tin of percussion caps – these contain a material which explodes when struck.*

▶ *A Colt patented bullet mould used for making home-made lead bullets.*

▼ *A six-shot single-action percussion revolver of .44 calibre, this Colt Army model was made in 1860.*

PRICE GUIDE **6**

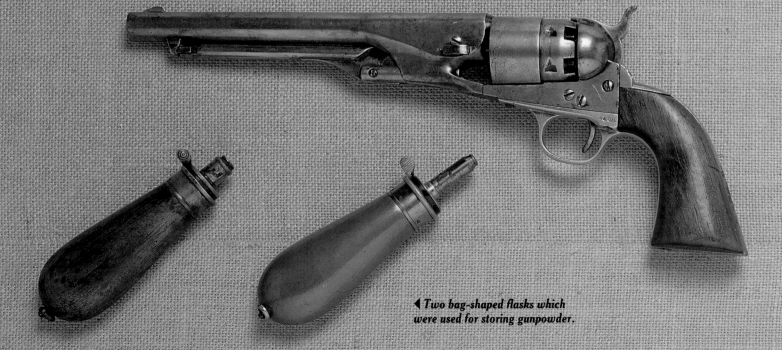

◀ *Two bag-shaped flasks which were used for storing gunpowder.*

PRICE GUIDE

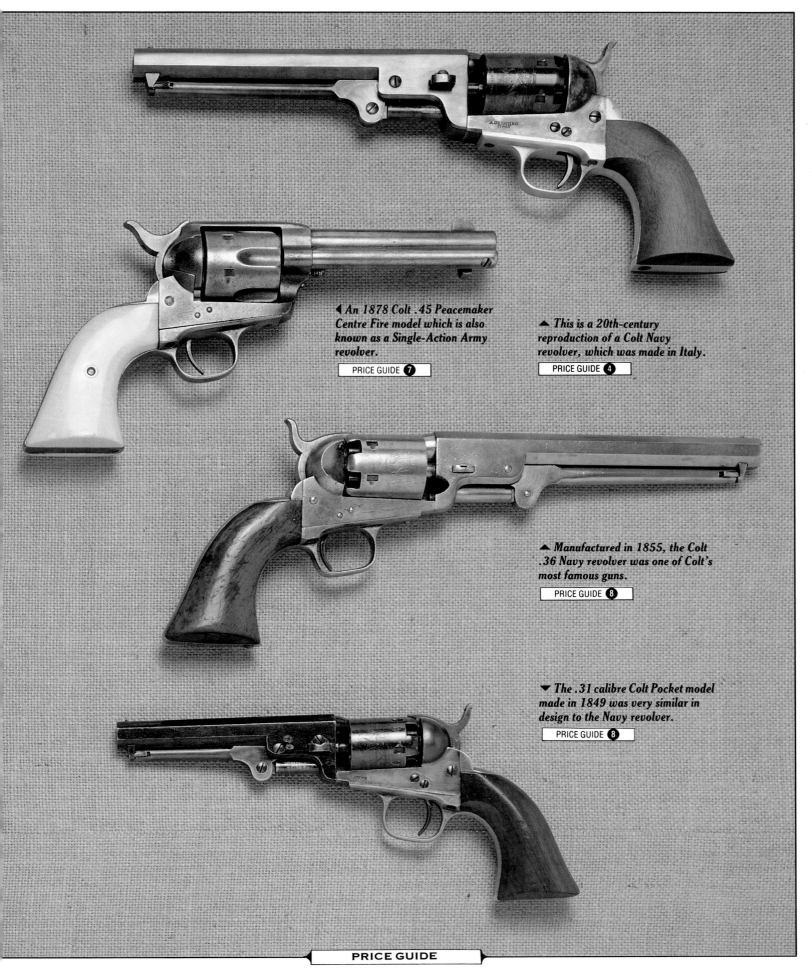

◀ *An 1878 Colt .45 Peacemaker Centre Fire model which is also known as a Single-Action Army revolver.*

PRICE GUIDE **7**

▲ *This is a 20th-century reproduction of a Colt Navy revolver, which was made in Italy.*

PRICE GUIDE **4**

▲ *Manufactured in 1855, the Colt .36 Navy revolver was one of Colt's most famous guns.*

PRICE GUIDE **8**

▼ *The .31 calibre Colt Pocket model made in 1849 was very similar in design to the Navy revolver.*

PRICE GUIDE **8**

PRICE GUIDE ▶

Colt Rifles

Colt Paterson revolving rifles were made in two basic types, those with an internal hammer and those with an external one. The Ring Lever model of 1837 had a ring mounted on the front of the frame which cocked the internal hammer, and was made as a .34 calibre and a .62 calibre. The main exception was the Patterson of 1837 which was a .50 calibre hammerless gun with twin-ring triggers, of which the forward one was implemented to cock the piece.

In 1839 the Paterson factory was producing a centre-hammer model in .56 calibre that was available in five-, six-, seven- or eight-chambered versions. In 1850, Dragoon-type models with side hammers were on the market – this hammer modification was a safety precaution, but by 1857 centre-hammer guns were back in fashion. These guns were chambered for six shots and came in a choice of the following three calibres: .36, .44 or .56.

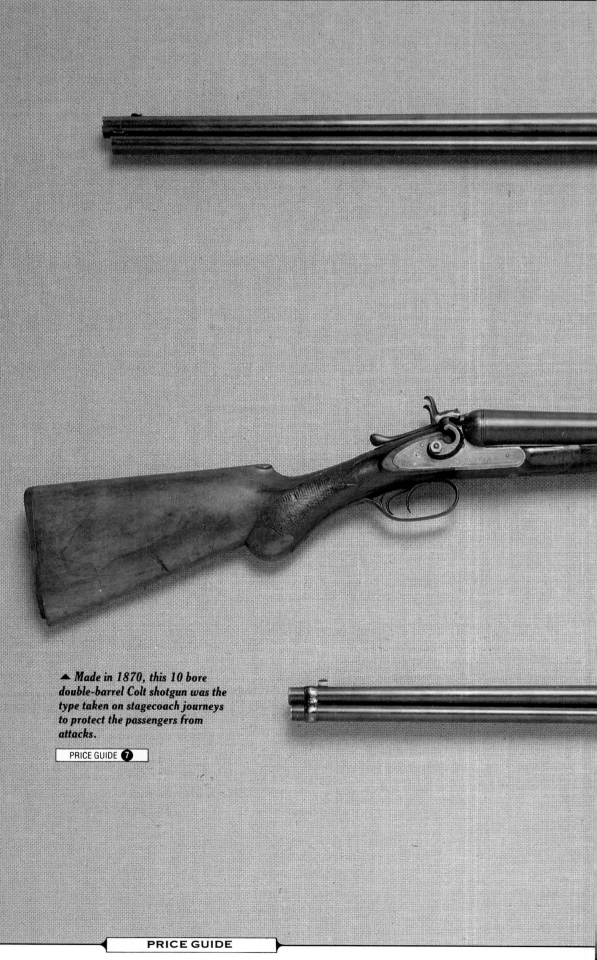

▲ *Made in 1870, this 10 bore double-barrel Colt shotgun was the type taken on stagecoach journeys to protect the passengers from attacks.*

PRICE GUIDE **7**

PRICE GUIDE

▲ *A .38 calibre Colt Lightning rifle made in 1870.*

PRICE GUIDE **7**

▼ *A .44 calibre Lightning Carbine – one of a group of weapons given to the Irish Rangers by the Guinness family during the Boer War.*

PRICE GUIDE **8**

PRICE GUIDE

Colt produced a wide range of weapons from the six-shot revolver to the Gatling gun but production can be split into three main groups: that from the Paterson factory in New Jersey, the Hartford factory in Connecticut and the Bessborough Place factory in London.

Paterson revolving rifles and revolvers are rare, particularly revolvers made for the Texas Rangers and most of the surviving weapons are in museums or private collections. The total number of revolvers produced at Paterson is under 3000, while about 2000 revolving rifles, carbines and shotguns were made there.

THE COLT NAVY REVOLVER

From the Hartford factory came the most famous Colt revolver of all, the .36 calibre Colt Navy, easily recognizable by the ships depicted on the chamber. The design was rolled on to the chamber by machine. Over 200,000 Navy revolvers were produced. There was a smaller revolver made called the 1848 Colt Pocket, built on similar lines with the exception of the design on the cylinder which was a stagecoach being held up by robbers. Over 30,000 Colt Pocket revolvers were made.

Special attention must be given to the Colt Walker and Dragoon models. These large revolvers, weighing over 4 lb (2 kg), are the priority on any Colt collector's list. The Walker was named after a captain in the Texas Rangers who, in a letter to Samuel Colt, praised the model, describing an incident in which it was used during the Indian Wars when 15 Texas Rangers attacked 80 Comanche Indians, killing half their number and putting the rest to flight. About 2000 Walker models were produced and approximately 20,000 of the Dragoon model.

THE ARMY REVOLVER

In 1860 Colt, in an effort to influence the US Military, introduced his new Army model, slightly larger than the Colt Navy. Its calibre was increased to .44. It was a successful idea, sold well and over 200,000

Flintlock Rifle

MADE AROUND 1800, THIS DOUBLE-BARRELLED FLINTLOCK RIFLE WAS DESIGNED FOR SHOOTING WILDFOWL. WITH THE FLINTLOCK FIRING MECHANISM, THE HAMMER WOULD STRIKE THE FLINT TO CREATE SPARKS — THIS MECHANISM WAS OFTEN AFFECTED BY THE WEATHER AND WAS GRADUALLY OVERTAKEN BY THE PERCUSSION CAP.

Component Parts

IN AN ATTEMPT TO GAIN A FOOTHOLD IN THE US MILITARY, COLT INTRODUCED HIS ARMY MODEL REVOLVER IN 1860. BASED ON THE POPULAR NAVY MODEL, IT WAS VERY SIMILAR IN DESIGN BUT WITH A .44 CALIBRE INSTEAD OF THE NAVY'S .36 CALIBRE.

① THE BARREL IS ROUND RATHER THAN OCTAGONAL WHICH WAS THE SHAPE FAVOURED FOR A NUMBER OF REVOLVERS.

② ALTHOUGH MADE ON THE SAME FRAME AS THE 1851 NAVY REVOLVER, THE CYLINDER IS REBATED.

③ SINGLE ACTION TRIGGER.

④ THE WALNUT GRIP IS SLIGHTLY LARGER AND IS A DIFFERENT SHAPE FROM PREVIOUS MODELS.

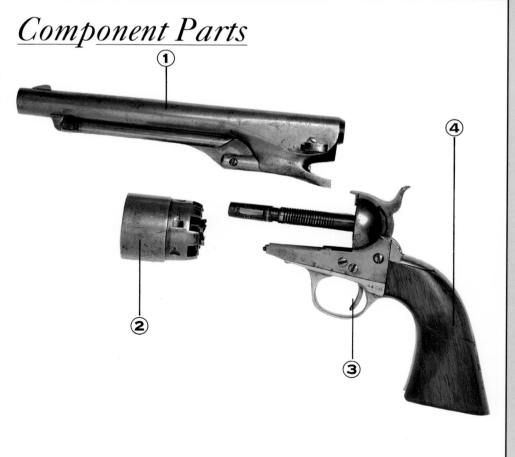

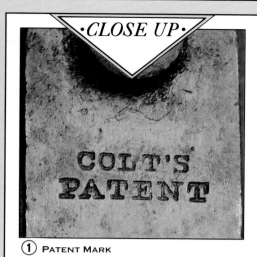

·CLOSE UP·

① **PATENT MARK**

① SAMUEL COLT TOOK OUT PATENTS ON HIS WEAPONS FROM 1835 ONWARDS.

② THE CORRECT MATCHING SERIAL NUMBERS ON A LONDON NAVY REVOLVER.

③ A COLT ARMY REVOLVER WITH .44 CALIBRE STAMPED ON THE FRAME.

④ THE FAMOUS COLT NAVY REVOLVER CAN ALWAYS BE IDENTIFIED BY THE SHIP DESIGN ON THE CHAMBER.

⑤ THE ADDRESS OF COLT'S LONDON FACTORY STAMPED ON THE BARREL OF A NAVY REVOLVER.

⑥ COLT'S NEW YORK ADDRESS FOUND ON THE BARREL OF THE 1848 POCKET REVOLVER.

② **SERIAL NUMBERS**

③ **CALIBRE**

④ **ENGRAVED SHIPS**

⑤ **LONDON ADDRESS**

⑥ **USA ADDRESS**

were produced. This and other models could also be supplied with a shoulder stock, coverting it to a carbine. There were other models produced in smaller quantities, for example Wells Fargo and police models and, of course, there were variations of many models made either experimentally or to specific customer requirements.

ANTIQUE PERCUSSION REVOLVERS
Due to the large number of weapons produced between 1847 and 1865, it is not difficult to find an antique percussion revolver by Colt. A London-cased Navy could be bought for between £1,200 and £2,000 depending on condition and uncased versions from £300 upwards.

A minor variation from normal production can increase value, in some instances to a large degree, and opportunities still exist

to find and buy a rare rifle or revolver.

In very recent times a first model 1853 sporting rifle was found covered in dirt and paint. Bought for a moderate sum, it was discovered to be a de luxe engraved model with 70 per cent of its original finish and with a value of £30,000!

POINTS TO WATCH
■ Beware of fakes. Colt weapons were copied in many countries, particularly Belgium and Spain.
■ Check to see whether the numbers match throughout the various parts of the weapon — due to Colt's manufacturing process, all parts were interchangeable, so a mis-match of numbers often occurs.
■ Condition is of paramount importance and if much of the original finish is still intact the value of the weapon is greatly increased.

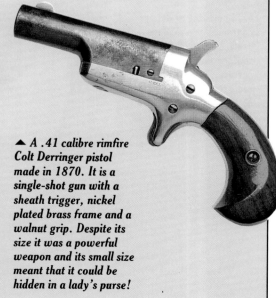

▲ *A .41 calibre rimfire Colt Derringer pistol made in 1870. It is a single-shot gun with a sheath trigger, nickel plated brass frame and a walnut grip. Despite its size it was a powerful weapon and its small size meant that it could be hidden in a lady's purse!*

Decoy Ducks

Bobbing gently on the river, the flotilla of
beautifully painted decoy ducks lured
unsuspecting birds within range of the
hunter's gun

Hunters have always had to rely on ingenuity
to catch their prey, and the use of decoys is
part of a repertoire of skills that includes
dressing up in animal skins to stalk, mimicking bird
calls, and laying traps. In fact the word 'decoy' is
said to have derived from the Dutch 'de kooi'
meaning trap. But although the use of tethered live
ducks as a lure dates back to dynastic Egypt, the
inanimate decoy duck is probably a New World
invention. In 1924 eleven canvasback duck decoys
more than 1000 years old were discovered in a
Nevada cave. Prototypes of the modern decoy, each
was fashioned from rush and feathers and equipped
with an anchor tether.

ABUNDANT WILDFOWL

When the first settlers arrived in Virginia, they
found wildfowl in teeming abundance on lake,
swamp and marsh while during the annual spring and
autumn migrations, geese, ducks, swans and shore
birds travelling from Maine to South Carolina
literally filled the skies.

Over the next three centuries the colonists
gradually improved on the Indian method of luring
birds, and developed more durable lightweight
wooden duck decoys. These would be positioned on
the water in a semicircle or a V-shape, downwind of
the hunter's stand or hide (all birds land into the
wind). Each decoy had its individual anchor and line
suspended from the keel or a loop attachment,
allowing it to bob and sway in the breeze. The line of
decoy ducks would be set down in naturalistic
groups, for example, two or more drakes courting the

▶ *The making of decoys*
continues as a modern
craft, both in their original
stylized forms and in a more
naturalistic style. This
realistic swan was carved
by Madison Mitchell, an
expert decoy maker from
Massachusetts, in 1956.

same duck, or a cluster of young drakes together.

Further sophisticated additions to a duck hunter's
'rig' included decoys of birds such as herons or gulls
which have the tendency to take off at the slightest
hint of danger, to lull the ducks into a false sense of
security (the so-called 'confidence decoy'), shorebird
decoys mounted on sticks to lure sea birds, and
'stick-ups' – painted silhouettes of ducks or geese
made of wood, sheet iron or tin which could be
pegged into marshy ground or harvested cornfields
near a river. Those who depended for food and extra
income on their success as hunters would occupy
themselves in the winter months carving new decoys,
forever improving on their modelling by accurate
observation of their intended prey.

By the 19th century industrialization had already
begun to have an irrevocable effect on hunting.
Firearms had metamorphosed into effective
assembly-line, rapid-fire repeater rifles and shotguns, while the development of the rail system,
freezer cars and urban growth meant that commercial

▲ *Decoy birds fetch*
particularly high prices if
they are genuine 19th-
century examples and if
they still have their original
paint. Probably all of this
selection was used for
hunting. Made from painted
tin or wood, they include
both floating and 'stick-up'
models of ducks, pigeons,
an ibis and other small
shore birds.

▶ *Hunting water birds was*
a popular pastime in the
time of artist Thomas
Eakins, as seen in this 1876
oil painting. It was a sport
for amateurs and skilled
hunters alike.

being manufactured at this time as well as tin shorebird decoys such as curlews, yellowlegs and dowitchers. Some decoys even included a decoy call that produced a realistic honking noise when activated by water currents.

CRAFTSMAN DECOYS

The craftsman-made decoy was fashioned from a variety of cheap materials including driftwood, cork, canvas and even papier-mâché, as well as local woods. Handsaws and other simple instruments were employed to carve the wood. In some areas, the body of the duck was hollowed out to facilitate buoyancy and portability; a small woodchip which rattled when shaken was sealed within to show that the decoy was hollow, and often the head was carved from a separate piece of wood. The decoy was painted with ordinary household gloss paint thinned down with petrol, or allowed to dry outside in damp conditions to eradicate shine. Finally, it was signed or branded with the owner's name to guard against potential loss.

Unlike manufacturers, most 19th-century craftsmen did not sign their own work. Yet decoys by such masters as Lothrop T. Holmes of Kingston, Massachusetts; Elmer Crowell based in Harwichport, Massachusetts; Bill Bowman of Lawrence, Long Island, New York, and John Glover of Duxburg, Massachusetts, are as recognizable to the dedicated collector as a Picasso or a Rembrandt are to a connoisseur of paintings.

Decoys varied according to the regions they came from, the local hunting methods and the skills of individual craftsmen. Wisconsin canvasbacks were carved with an erect head and jutting breast to facilitate their journey through river ice, while in the Delaware river area, particular care was taken with the fashioning and decoration of the head and wing feathers of decoy waterfowl.

The success of the new mass-market approach to hunting inevitably carried the seeds of its own demise. Gunners in the Chesapeake Bay area, for example, shooting from a sinkbox or floating hide, using a 'rig' of 100 or so decoys, and heavy 160 lb (73 kg) guns capable of firing up to two pounds of

hunting suddenly became a lucrative business. One hunter of the period announced that 'no first class hotel or restaurant was considered worthy of the name that didn't furnish frequent game dinners.'

DECOY MANUFACTURERS

Factories were set up to cater for the new breed of 'market gunners'. Large manufacturers such as H. A. Stevens of Weedsport, New York; Wildfowler of Sayebrook, New York; Dodge and Petersen, and Masons, both of Detroit, successfully merchandized hand-finished wooden decoys at an affordable nine to 12 dollars per dozen. Mason's Decoy Factory continued to produce superbly carved and painted shorebird decoys until 1925. Simple boxed field kits were marketed for the amateur by firms such as Kirkwood Bros. of Boston. They carried powder and lead shot for hand-loaded shells, with crude 'stick-ups' and a decoy whistle.

The first rubber decoys appeared in 1867. Metal models designed to float on wooden bases were also

shot over a large area, could be individually responsible for killing over 500 ducks in one day. By the end of the 19th century the Labrador duck was extinct and the wood duck, which the American naturalist Audubon had witnessed travelling in flocks in the 1820s, had become an endangered species. The Migratory Bird Act of 1918 finally put an end to such wholesale slaughter.

Decoys continued to be made but on a very limited scale. However it was not until the publication of Joel Barber's *Wild Fowl Decoys* in 1934 that the decoy began to be appreciated for its aesthetic and decorative qualities. The last two decades in particular have seen its appreciation as a unique collector's item, a piece of folk art which combines aesthetic beauty with a romantic nostalgia for a vanished past.

CONDITION AND PRICE

The price of decoy ducks does not depend on good condition; indeed the decoy collector will expect to pay a higher price for an example that has clearly seen some practical use. Catalogues for the important sales usually held in the United States append the letters 'OP' to the descriptions of some decoys, indicating that the original paintwork still adheres. Repainting is not recommended.

A number of examples were imported into the United Kingdom, more particularly Scotland, during the 19th century, while British-made decoys

dating back to Georgian times have very occasionally appeared on the market. Collecting early decoys can be expensive in a rapidly rising market which is sufficiently lucrative to attract large numbers of forgeries. This is also reflected by the growing interest in the more affordable anchor weights as collectables.

Some collectors concentrate on modern decoys: 20th-century craftsmen such as the Ward Brothers of Crisfield, Chesapeake ('Wildfowl Counterfeiters in Wood'), have continued the tradition, making decorative decoys for a burgeoning collectors' market in traditional or naturalistic styles. Today's investment may prove tomorrow's heirloom.

▲ *These Canada goose decoys are fine examples of practical, stylized folk art. Carved from wood, c.1849, by Captain Charles Osgood of Salem, Mass., each goose was made in three pieces and then joined together. Great attention was given to carving the head. The complete goose was then sandpapered down and painted in naturalistic colours.*

·PRICE GUIDE· ≫   **DECOY DUCKS**

The highest price paid to date for a decoy duck is $319,000 for an exquisite preening pintail, carved by Elmer Crowell at the end of the 19th century. Even factory-made decoys can fetch several thousand dollars if the quality of the hand finishing is high enough. Ultimately prices are dependent on the quality of the piece,

with decoys from the top end of the market finding their way to the better American auctions. The rarity of 19th-century decoys which have not already found their way into collections also accounts for the high prices. English decoys of the period are still reasonably cheap by American standards, ranging from £200-£400.

The Victorian Billiard Room

As the popularity of billiards increased, the Victorians took great pleasure in recreating a relaxed club atmosphere in their own homes

To have a room totally devoted to the game of billiards would today be regarded by most as an indulgence only for the super-rich. A century ago, however, houses with their own billiard rooms were by no means exceptional. By the year 1870 billiards was such an integral part of the wealthy Englishman's way of life, that only a particularly puritan spirit would have considered building a country house without one.

The Victorian billiard room was, predictably, a male preserve where many of the formalities observed in the rest of the house were excused. Here, smoking was not frowned upon and gentlemen could enjoy an after-dinner port in their shirt sleeves. In this room, frequently built as an extension to the main part of the house, the master could give free rein to his own taste. High vaulted ceilings were a popular feature of purpose-built billiard rooms while carved wood panelling gave a sumptuous air to an otherwise sparsely furnished room.

Adjustable lights hung over the centrally placed table were an important feature of the billiard room.

It was not only at home that billiards was popular: in clubs up and down the country special rooms were devoted to the game. Much further afield, in the far-flung outposts of the Empire, billiard rooms formed the focus of club life and helped to re-create one well-loved aspect of the Old Country.

▼ A purpose-built billiard room was the ideal of most Victorian enthusiasts. A glass roof allowed ample and even lighting for daytime play, while a blazing fire kept the cold at bay. This engraving shows a design for a fully-equipped billiard room, complete with cabinet scoreboard and bench seat on a raised dais for use by spectators or players.

If it was true that 'to play billiards well was the sign of an ill-spent youth', then the saintly Prince Albert was the one to blame for corrupting the young men of England. It was his love of the game that persuaded Queen Victoria to have tables at the various royal residences and with the royal seal of approval the billiard room became as essential in the large country house as the morning room or the library. In time, town houses and suburban villas also had extensions built on to accommodate the Victorian gentleman's passion for the game, but it was in country houses during the hunting and shooting seasons that the billiard room enjoyed its golden age.

ROOM FOR THE RICH

The building of a sizeable annexe simply to house a billiard table was, of course, an enormous expense, which many a mortgaged family estate could not afford. Gentlemen in straitened circumstances were obliged to set up a table in one of the larger existing rooms, the library or the front hall. The latter arrangement was, it appears, most unsatisfactory: 'The game is constantly interrupted by traffic to the front door; men cannot play in their shirt-sleeves; and their tobacco smoke rises to the upper rooms and passage ways.' Late at night some men did play in their waistcoats and shirt-sleeves, but if a lady made an unexpected entrance, they would all rush to put on their coats. Consequently, when money became available, a purpose-built billiard room was a high priority.

A single-storey extension would usually be built

on at the end of a suitable corridor, joined to the house at one of its narrow sides. To give the exterior of the annexe an appearance of antiquity, it was often fitted with square-paned, leaded windows set in impressive stone mullions. If possible, there would be windows in all three external walls to give an even light, the room ending in a bow window, in front of which was a raised dais for use by spectators. If the

room was wide enough, a further dais ran along the wall opposite the fireplace.

During the first half of Victoria's reign the decoration of billiard rooms was conservative: high oak panelling was hung with family portraits, then mounted above the panelling would be a row of hunting trophies, the illusion of an ancestral hall being completed by a mock-beamed ceiling and heavy plush curtains.

SMOKING-ROOM TRAPPINGS

In new houses, however, the room began to develop a character of its own. From about 1860 large country houses were frequently built with one wing housing a suite of rooms dedicated to masculine pastimes; the smoking room, the billiard room and the gun room. As a result of their proximity, the trappings of the smoking room began to invade the billiard room, especially when 'Moorish' furnishings

and decoration became fashionable in the 1870s. The chimney-piece might now be an oriental fantasy of blue and white tiles or carved stone arabesques and pinnacles, and the impression that you were entering some Eastern potentate's harem was reinforced by an enormous fretted wooden screen, with as many as 12 leaves, which stood in front of the double doors, so that players would not be disturbed by people coming in.

Further oriental touches could be added to the room by having divans ranged along the spectators' dais instead of the more usual soft leather banquettes and small hexagonal occasional tables for drinks. The large fire screen, used when the fireplace was closed up for the summer, might also be decorated with Moorish motifs, but was equally likely to sport Japanese dragons. These were also popular on jars used to house potted-plants, which, along with brass spittoons and sand-filled ash trays, gave the room the

▲ *Liquid refreshment was always on hand; bottles were often stored in a lead-lined cellaret. This one is a Georgian piece.*

Billiard Accessories

CLUBS, HOTELS AND PUBS, AS WELL AS PRIVATE HOUSES, HAVE HELPED TO PRESERVE A GOOD NUMBER OF BILLIARD ACCESSORIES, RANGING FROM COMPLETE SETS OF SOLID IVORY BILLIARD BALLS TO THE ELABORATELY INLAID CUES AND INTRIGUING CUE RESTS USED BY PLAYERS DURING THE LAST CENTURY. MANY ARE OF GREAT INTEREST TO COLLECTORS TODAY.

WOODEN SCOREBOARDS EQUIPPED WITH DIALS OR SLIDES ARE ATTRACTIVE BUT MOSTLY INCOMPREHENSIBLE TO MODERN PLAYERS BECAUSE THEY INCLUDE MARKING BOARDS FOR LIFE POOL. IN THIS GAME, A PLAYER HAD THREE 'LIVES' AND EACH TIME HIS BALL WAS POTTED HE LOST ONE. THE LAST PLAYER LEFT 'ALIVE' TOOK THE POOL, THE STAKES FOR

WHICH WERE SOMETIMES INSERTED IN THE SCOREBOARD.

PRIVATE HOUSES OFTEN BOASTED A SPLENDIDLY CARVED CABINET WITH A MANTEL-SHELF AND SCOREBOARD ABOVE IT, WHICH STOOD AGAINST THE WALL WITH AN EQUALLY IMPRESSIVE CUE-RACK. IN THE FIRST HALF OF THE 19TH CENTURY, OLD-FASHIONED MACES, SOME WITH IVORY HEADS AND SIGHT-LINES TO HELP THE PLAYERS' AIM, STOOD SIDE BY SIDE WITH THE CUES. LATER, THEY WERE REPLACED BY A SELECTION OF IMPLEMENTS EASILY RECOGNIZABLE AS THE ANCESTORS OF MODERN RESTS AND 'SPIDERS'. ANTIQUE OBJECTS THAT MIGHT NOT BE RECOGNIZED TODAY INCLUDE RECTANGULAR IRONS FOR SMOOTHING THE CLOTH AND HAND-HELD SCORERS, FOR USE BY SPECTATORS DURING A GAME.

▼ ANTIQUE BILLIARDS EQUIPMENT GIVES A FASCINATING INSIGHT INTO THE HISTORY OF THE GAME AND SOME PIECES CAN BE SURPRISINGLY VALUABLE. BILLIARD BALLS WERE ORIGINALLY MADE OF IVORY — TO SUPPLY BRITAIN FOR JUST ONE YEAR REQUIRED THE SLAUGHTER OF 12,000 ELEPHANTS.

RILEY'S
BILLIARD TABLES

A Billiard Table for the Home—

E. J. Riley, Ltd., Abbey Mills, Accrington
London Showrooms 147, Aldersgate Street, E.C.

feel of a club or hotel. The wooden floor was usually left bare except for strips or 'runners' of good Turkey carpet arranged around the table.

Whatever the style of peripheral furnishings, the essential centrepiece of the room was unmistakeably English. Although the size of billiard tables was not officially standardized until 1892, serious billiards was always played on a surface which was around 12 × 6 feet (3.6 × 1.8 metres), so today's players would have felt quite at home lining up a shot on a Victorian table. They would, however, have been more than a little disconcerted by the 'rumble' of the ivory balls, as they rolled across the thick slate bed.

Old players could still remember the days when the beds of billiard tables had been made of wood. The first slate-bed table was made for White's Club in 1826 by John Thurston, who went on to revolutionize the British billiards trade. In order to reduce 'rumble', beds were made thicker and thicker, until some tables had to bear the weight of several inches of slate. The underframing of such tables entered the province of the engineer and their six or eight legs became massive architectural columns.

Thurston's became the leading suppliers of billiard tables and pioneered most of the century's technological innovations. They were, for example, the first to experiment with rubber cushions. Previously, layers of felt stuffing had been used to make the balls rebound. Unfortunately ordinary india rubber was hardly any better as it lost its bounce in cold weather and the cushions had to be warmed by means of a set of six specially shaped pans of hot water. But Thurston's overcame this

▲ *Although the vast majority of players were men, some women also enjoyed the game. They would not join the men in the billiard room after dinner, but on wet afternoons bold young ladies found that the game of billiards offered splendid opportunities for a little mild flirtation.*

problem when they started using vulcanized rubber in 1845 – this retained it resilience in low temperatures and was proudly marketed as 'Frost Proof'.

BILLIARDS, PYRAMIDS AND POOL
In the genealogy of games, billiards is probably a distant indoor cousin of croquet, both having evolved from the medieval French game of *paille-maille*. It is certain that billiards was originally played on a grassy plot out-of-doors, but there is no record of when and why it moved indoors on to an artificial turf of green cloth. In the late 17th century, by which time the game had been played on a table for over 200 years, billiards still involved the use of a hoop and a post and the two balls were struck with a wooden 'mace'.

In the 18th century the game changed rapidly. The French, having discarded the hoop and post, also dispensed with pockets, condemning their

▲ *Not everyone had the means to buy a full-sized billiard table. Miniature tables which could be set up on larger tables were advertised as a cheaper alternative. The dining rooms of many suburban homes must have doubled as a games room around the turn of the century.*

players to do nothing but score cannons. Even so, they made two vital contributions to the English game. The first was the red ball, the second when they turned their maces round and started using the wrong end, the *queue,* hence the English 'cue'.

The English persevered with the mace well into the 19th century, using the cue principally for tricky shots from near the cushion, but, with the introduction (also from France) of the leather cut-tip, the superiority of the cue on the new slate-bedded tables was undeniable and the game took on its modern appearance. The only relic of the medieval mace is now the flattened side of the butt. Nevertheless, many Victorians continued to hit the ball with the butt end, playing one-handed, rather than use a rest.

Billiards, which was hardly changed since the mid 19th century, was the most popular game with Victorians, but there were light-hearted alternatives to the serious three-ball game. The triangle now used to arrange the reds in snooker was first made for the game of pyramids, essentially snooker without any coloured balls, while today's coloured balls originally featured in 'life pool', an all-against-all game for as many as 12 players. Snooker was invented by bored soldiers in India, who in the 1870s started adding coloured balls from the life pool game to the reds used in pyramids, but it was not until the beginning of this century that a serious attempt was made to codify the rules.

The keenest billiards players were usually military or ex-military men. For most people the game merely provided a little not-too-energetic recreation to assist in the digestion of a copious dinner, but the serious player took himself off to clubs frequented by professionals and gamblers. When the London season was over and he was doing the rounds of hospitable country seats, he could amaze his fellow guests with his strokes and pocket a few wagers.

SERVICING AND SERVANTS

When the family were not in residence, country house billiard rooms were often locked up for long periods. When it was announced that the master and mistress were expected with a large house-party, a footman would remove the cover from the table and discover that the cloth was threadbare and torn or spotted with drips from the oil-lamps. The cushions might also need replacing, the balls might be chipped and the cues warped and tipless. Immediately the man from Thurston's (or whichever company had supplied the table) would be summoned to put matters right before the guests arrived.

The day-to-day maintenance of the billiard table and equipment was usually the responsibility of one of the manservants. If a serious match was to take place after dinner, a footman might be employed to act as marker, giving the occasion the solemnity of a competition in a club, while on evenings when there was a convivial party of gentlemen in the room, the butler, whose pantry was usually situated close by, would be called to replenish the players' supply of port and brandy. Unless they were given permission to retire to bed, butler and footman were expected to stay up until the players had finished their game. The gentlemen were as well looked after as in the smartest London club.

▲ *The masculine character of the Victorian billiard room was emphasized in both furnishings and ornaments. This large porcelain vase, one of a pair designed in 1872, is decorated in the popular Japanese style.*

THEN AND NOW
Table Lighting

THE ESSENCE OF GOOD LIGHTING FOR BILLIARD TABLES WAS THAT IT SHOULD CAST NO SHADOW. THIS HAD BEEN IMPOSSIBLE IN THE DAYS OF CANDLELIGHT BUT EVEN BY MID-VICTORIAN TIMES, OIL LAMP RESERVOIRS WERE STILL CAUSING SIZEABLE SHADOWS. GAS, ON THE OTHER HAND, GAVE AN EVEN LIGHT AND IN TOWNS WHERE IT WAS AVAILABLE MAGNIFICENT GAS CHANDELIERS HUNG FROM THE CEILINGS OF BILLIARD ROOMS BY MEANS OF ORNATE METAL TUBES. IN CLUBS, THE SHADES WERE USUALLY SIMPLE METAL CONES OR PYRAMID SHAPES DESIGNED TO REFLECT AS MUCH LIGHT AS POSSIBLE, BUT IN PRIVATE HOUSES CONFECTIONS OF BRIGHTLY COLOURED SILK FRINGED WITH TASSELS WERE OFTEN FAVOURED.

▲ *Six-light pendant gas chandeliers became standard by end of the 19th century.*

▲ *Reproduction Tiffany shades provide an attractive option in a modern setting.*

Playing Cards

The Victorians' passion for games led to a tremendous increase in the production of playing cards, and collectors delight in the many beautiful designs that survive today

Games have played an important part in recreational life since civilization began, and one of the most popular and enduring creations was the pack of cards. No-one knows where or when playing cards were invented, although they are thought to have originated in China or India. They first appeared in Europe in the Middle Ages. In 1377 a German monk wrote, 'a certain game called the game of cards has come to us this year'. However, it was almost a century later before there was any evidence of playing cards in England. The first cards were hand-painted and because they were expensive, cards was the game of the rich.

EARLY CARDS

European packs have always had four suits, although the subjects of the suits have varied at different times and in different countries. The suits of playing cards which form the basis of the designs we know today most likely originated in the French town of Rouen, where there was a thriving card industry. The 16th and 17th century Jacks, Queens and Kings are known as court cards, as the figures are depicted wearing French court dress.

By the 17th century the playing of cards was well established in England. The Worshipful Company of Makers of Playing Cards was granted a royal charter in 1628 and all card makers were required to identify themselves on the ace of spades and to

A selection of cards from a pack by Charles Goodall issued in 1900 to mark the new century. The court cards honour European monarchs and statesmen.

▼ *Many Victorian gentlemen played cards and gambled with fervour. As gambling was frowned upon by the church and much of society, gentlemen often had to restrict their pleasure and play away from home at their club.*

register their identifying marks with the company.

During the middle of the 17th century thousands of card packs were destroyed by the Puritans who disapproved of gambling, but with the restoration of Charles II in 1660 card playing flourished again. A century later, in 1773, card games were so popular that Boswell, in *The Journal of a Tour of the Hebrides* lamented, 'I am sorry I have not learnt to play at cards. It is very useful in life; it generates kindness and consolidates society'.

VICTORIAN PLAYING CARDS

The Victorians were keen card players and card games were popular with men, women and children of all social classes. During this period mass-production ensured that cards were cheap; new games were developed and the design of the playing card was irrevocably altered.

One of the most important changes in the design of the playing card was printing the values of the court cards at both the top and bottom. Before the mid-19th century the court cards illustrated a single standing figure. Double-headed cards had been made on the Continent since the mid-18th century, but British players steadfastly refused to change from the traditional design until the 1850s when the important card makers of Goodall and De La Rue both printed double-headed packs.

Other changes appeared later in the century. From around 1880 the value of the card was printed in the top left and bottom right corners; this allowed the player to see the whole of his hand without spreading it very wide. Machine-cutting replaced hand-cutting and the corners of the cards were rounded; square corners had damaged easily. Cards became thinner and more flexible so that they were more easily shuffled. It was also about this time that the joker appeared in the English pack. Initially it was an extra, blank card used in the American game

Transformation Cards

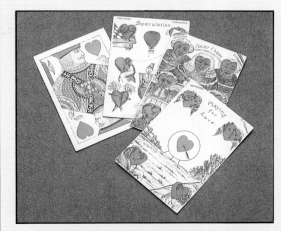

TRANSFORMATION CARDS, WHERE THE NUMBER OF HEARTS, CLUBS, SPADES AND DIAMONDS WAS INCORPORATED INTO A SPECIFIC DESIGN, BECAME POPULAR EARLY IN THE 19TH CENTURY AND MANY ATTRACTIVE PACKS WERE DESIGNED.

The court cards in this 1897 set by Charles Goodall depict famous English monarchs and their consorts with Victoria on the reverse side.

Fortune-telling Cards

◄ TAROT CARDS, NOW USED FOR FORTUNE TELLING, WERE ORIGINALLY DESIGNED FOR A CARD GAME.

► MANY VICTORIAN WOMEN BELIEVED IN THE POWERS OF FORTUNE TELLERS, AND OFTEN PAID MONEY TO LEARN NEWS OF A FAR-AWAY SWEETHEART.

MEDIEVAL FORTUNE TELLERS SOON ADOPTED CARDS AS A MEANS OF PLYING THEIR TRADE AND CARDS REPLACED DICE AS A METHOD OF PREDICTING THE FUTURE. AT FIRST ORDINARY PLAYING CARDS WERE USED. THE CUSTOMER CHOSE A CARD FROM THE PACK AND THE FORTUNE TELLER EXPLAINED ITS SIGNIFICANCE OR THE PERSON DRAWING THE CARD REFERRED TO A FORTUNE-TELLING BOOK.

AT THE END OF THE 17TH CENTURY THE FIRST FORTUNE-TELLING CARDS APPEARED. IN EFFECT THE INFORMATION IN FORTUNE-TELLING BOOKS WAS NOW TRANSFERRED TO THE SURFACE OF THE CARDS.

THE NEXT DEVELOPMENT IN FORTUNE-TELLING CARDS CAME IN THE 18TH CENTURY WHEN THE ANSWER WAS NOT GIVEN TO A SINGLE CARD BUT TO A COMBINATION OF CARDS DRAWN. AT ABOUT THE SAME TIME FRENCH FORTUNE TELLERS STARTED TO USE CARDS FROM THE MARSEILLE TAROT PACK. ALTHOUGH TODAY THE TAROT PACK IS ASSOCIATED WITH PREDICTING THE FUTURE, BEFORE THE 18TH CENTURY IT WAS USED TO PLAY CARD GAMES.

·PRICE GUIDE· CARDS AND ACCESSORIES

Playing cards and accessories from the 19th and early 20th century are now highly collectable, and perfect decks of cards are becoming increasingly hard to find.

▼ *Mother-of-pearl gaming chips, two carved and embellished in the shape of fish.*

PRICE GUIDE ❸

► *'Great Mogul' playing cards manufactured in Belgium. The court cards depict standing figures.*

PRICE GUIDE ❸

►► *Early 20th-century imitation-ivory dice of good quality, sold in pairs.*

PRICE GUIDE ❶

▼ *Playing cards by Charles Goodall with rounded corners, produced in the 1900s.*

PRICE GUIDE ❷

of euchre, but soon cardmakers were designing their own distinctive jokers.

Some of the most interesting cards made in the 19th century, up until about 1880, were transformation cards, so-called because the suit signs formed part of a picture. Each card in the pack illustrated something different. Because of the amount of work it took to produce a new pack, pirating was rife.

GAMES AND GAMING

Many card games played in Victorian Britain are still played today. Whist, with its many variations, such as solo and boston, was universally popular. Towards the end of the 19th century it was played less often as bridge gradually gained popularity.

Patience had the advantage that no other player was required. Variations abounded and several games were played with 32-card packs, which were made by removing the twos, threes, fours, fives and sixes. Another game with 32 cards was euchre, which was played by two to six players.

Other popular games included bezique, ecarté and piquet, all of which were for two players, and loo, a gambling game for any number of players.

Children's card games and children's packs, many of them educational, flourished at this time. Old maid, happy families and snap were all popular. There were also zoo cards, cards on geography, monarchs, Roman emperors and astronomy.

If, to add excitement to the game, gambling was a feature, counters or chips would be used instead of money. At the end of the last round, debts would be settled in cash. Gaming chips were made in a variety of materials, including mother-of-pearl and ivory.

Imitation silver coins were embellished with decorations such as the monarch's head or an eagle. 'Spade guineas' were imitation guineas embossed with a spade design.

Not everyone, of course, approved of gambling. And those that tolerated gambling for small amounts often condemned playing for high stakes. According to W. A. Chatto, the author of *Facts and Speculations on the Origin and History of Playing Cards,* the latter was a positive evil to society. Even more sinful than gambling was cheating. This was the worst thing a gentleman could do, and a cheat would be ostracized from society.

BUYING CARDS

When buying old cards, check that the cards are in good condition without torn or dogeared corners. Cards are highly perishable and are quickly worn and discarded. For this reason, hardly any cards survive from before 1600 and even 17th and 18th century packs can cost several hundred pounds. When looking at 18th and 19th century packs make sure that the pack has not been reassembled from miscellaneous cards. Check the details of the printer's imprint and the quality of the printing; it should be the same throughout the pack. Packs still in the original wrappers and boxes are more valuable than loose packs. Early De La Rue packs are highly collectable as are early 19th century packs by the European makers Grimaud of Paris and Piatnik of Vienna. Complete packs of 19th century children's games in good condition, such as happy families, are also fairly rare and make an excellent subject for a collection.

▼ *Pope Joan, a popular card game in Victorian times, was played with a 52-card pack minus the eight of diamonds (known as the 'Pope Joan') and a revolving circular tray containing eight compartments. Any number of players could participate, each starting with 30 counters.*

PRICE GUIDE ❸

▼ *Edwardian cardboard and tin dice shaker, widely used to throw dice in games of chance.*

PRICE GUIDE ❶

▼ *'Great Mogul' playing cards, c. 1890. The court card images show a similarity to those on modern packs.*

PRICE GUIDE ❷

Chess Pieces

The evolution of the basic designs and the countless artistic variations on their forms make chessmen a subject of never-ending fascination

English chess in the mid-18th century was not in very good health. Georgian society was more attracted to the gregarious pleasures of the card table, and dedicated chess-players, who preferred the quiet of the library to the chatter of the drawing room, were regarded by many as being slightly eccentric.

Dr Johnson in his famous *Dictionary of the English Language* (1755) defined chess as 'a nice and abstruse game in which two sets of puppets are moved in opposition to each other.' In 18th-century Europe the 'puppets' were often made less for play than as pretty ornaments. Knights turned into seahorses and queens into mermaids, as sets were made in such beautiful and extravagant materials as silver, Meissen porcelain, alabaster, porphyry, amber and even hollow Venetian glass.

A REVIVAL OF INTEREST

On the whole, chess was more popular on the Continent, and it was a Frenchman who revived serious English interest in the game. François André Philidor was not only the finest chess-player of the age, but also a distinguished composer. Whenever his musi-

Early Chess Piece

EARLY CHESSMEN FREQUENTLY RESEMBLE MINIATURE SCULPTURES. THIS ELABORATE ENGLISH PIECE, PROBABLY A KING, IS OF IVORY, AND DATES FROM THE 13TH CENTURY.

cal career was in the doldrums, he turned to chess to make a living.

He first visited England in 1747, but it was in the 1770s and 80s, when he took to spending the entire season from February to June in London, that his influence started to inspire English players to higher things. At new chess clubs like the exclusive Parsloe's in St James's Street he amazed onlookers by playing three simultaneous games (two of them blindfold), an easy feat for many modern chess masters, but enough to make Philidor the toast of London.

Ordinary English wooden or ivory pieces used for playing chess in the mid-18th century had changed remarkably little since the Elizabethan age. The revival of interest in the game and its spread to a much wider section of society was accompanied by a proliferation in the shapes and styles of chessmen.

At the same time sets started to be imported from India, Burma and China, not just as occasional rarities, but on a regular commercial basis. Many English (and continental) firms in the 19th century arranged to have their designs manufactured in India, where skilled ivory-turning and carving was much cheaper. As a result, many chess sets of the period show a remarkable cross-fertilization of Eastern and Western decorative traditions.

Such cross-fertilization was nothing new in the history of chess, which originated in India and gradually spread West. Its origins are obscure, but it existed in a form that was the direct ancestor of today's game by about the 6th or 7th century AD, when it passed from India to Persia. From Persia it spread throughout the Islamic world and thence to medieval Europe.

Originally the pieces had been representational, but the Moslems, being forbidden to make images of men or animals, had used simple abstract shapes. The Europeans, having given the pieces new names, gave them lifelike qualities to go with them – quite different ones in most cases from the Persian and Indian originals. The Persian elephant, for example, became the English bishop and the French *fou* (fool). Finally, in the late-15th century, European players altered the moves of the bishop and queen, giving us, more or less, the game we know today. Boards had originally been uncoloured, but the familiar checkered pattern was in use by

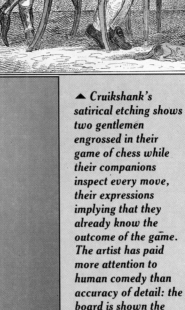

the 13th century and still is today.

Throughout the history of the game, the design of chess pieces has been governed by three contradictory considerations: sculptural realism, decorative architectural detail and standardized abstraction. Realistic sets were seldom intended for actual play; they were made for presentation to important people or as commemorative souvenirs. The Napoleonic Wars, for example, inspired a

▲ *Cruikshank's satirical etching shows two gentlemen engrossed in their game of chess while their companions inspect every move, their expressions implying that they already know the outcome of the game. The artist has paid more attention to human comedy than accuracy of detail: the board is shown the wrong way round, and the number of pieces depicted is incorrect.*

◀ *The opening moves have just been made in a game of chess, which is being played with antique chessmen: the finely carved ivory pieces were made in England in the early 19th century. The great appeal of old chessmen is that they are highly attractive pieces that can still be put to practical use.*

spate of sets in which the white and red (at this time more common than black) kings were busts or statuettes of the Duke of Wellington and Napoleon.

TRADITIONAL DESIGNS

Every European country developed its own traditional designs, using different combinations of columns, balusters, discs, reels and finials. Many Austrian and German sets from the 17th to the 19th century were constructed of characteristic tiers of pierced, spiky crowns or 'crow's nests', and often feature a double-headed knight.

English and French pieces of the late 18th and 19th centuries come in a great variety of different designs. In England the main choice lay between sturdy Old English pieces on firm, roughly hemispherical bases and the more decorative 'barleycorn' sets, balanced precariously on a slender baluster rising from a flat disc. French styles ranged from the endearing, dumpy 'St George' pieces to the slender, abstract 'Directoire' sets, where the knight was not represented by a horse's head, much to the annoyance of players unused to that design.

Eventually serious players grew tired of hearing the excuse 'I thought it was a bishop': the time had come for a standard set, at least for serious tournament play. The elegant, well-balanced pieces which eventually won this honour were designed by Nathaniel Cooke, manufactured by John Jaques of London, and in 1849 given the blessing of Howard Staunton, the autocratic overlord of English chess.

Though legend has it that Staunton refused to play with any other pieces, they did not receive instant recognition. In any case, makers in every European country (including Britain) continued to produce traditional designs and to import ornate, decorative pieces from the Far East.

Bone, Wood and Ceramic Pieces

A cheap alternative to ivory was bone, and many chess sets were turned and carved in sheep's bone in the late 18th and early 19th centuries. Some of the finest can now be as valuable as similar ivory sets, notably those carved by French prisoners of war in Napoleonic times. However, the material used in the vast majority of sets was, of course, wood. The best wooden sets used boxwood for the white pieces and ebony for the black. Top-quality 'Staunton' sets have been made in weighted boxwood and ebony ever since John Jaques started producing them. In cheaper sets both red (or black) and white pieces were in boxwood.

At the upper end of the market, every conceivable material has been used for unusual or luxury sets. Chessmen have been cast in bronze and silver ever since the Renaissance. With silver chessmen, one of the sets was gilded to distinguish the colours of the two players.

Pottery and porcelain have also long been favourite mate-rials for amusing chess sets. Many made in faience in Rouen and other northern French towns found their way to Eng-land, one side decorated pre-dominantly in blue, the other in red. They were usually sold with a charming pottery board on which to display them. Of porcelain sets, the most cele-brated, in the eyes of English collectors, is the one designed by John Flaxman in 1783 and made in Wedgwood's jasper ware. The models for the king and queen were John Kemble and his sister Sarah Siddons as Macbeth and Lady Macbeth. Price guides relate to sets, not the individual figures.

▲ *Seven pieces from an early 19th-century black and white Royal Worcester chess set based on an original Wedgwood set designed by the sculptor John Flaxman. The figures are inspired by Shakespeare's play* Macbeth.

PRICE GUIDE **8**

▶ *Six pieces from a light blue and black glazed ceramic chess set made by the Castleford Pottery in the 1820s. The figures are shown wearing modern costume.*

PRICE GUIDE **8**

PRICE GUIDE

▼ *These wooden chess pieces were made in Ireland for the English nobility around the year 1800. Different coloured woods are used for the two sides.*

PRICE GUIDE **8**

▼ *Pieces from a late 18th-century Central European bone chess set. The 'crows'-nests' are typical features of continental chessmen.*

PRICE GUIDE **7**

▼ *A surprisingly modern-looking early 19th-century horn chess set, made in France.*

PRICE GUIDE **6**

PRICE GUIDE

Ivory Pieces

Ivory has always been a favourite substance for making small sculptural objects that must be handled to be fully appreciated, and it is the classic material for chess pieces. The finest ivory for chessmen is that of the African elephant, cream-coloured, but turning yellow with age and gratifyingly smooth to the touch. The most beautifully carved pieces, however, tend to come from the East, where the whiter ivory of the Indian elephant was used. Among the very finest pieces are Chinese kings and queens in Mandarin costume, mounted on a pedestal in the shape of a hollow fretwork ball. This ball contains three, four, even as many as seven concentric balls, all floating freely inside.

It was usual with ivory sets to leave the white pieces plain and stain the opposing pieces red or green. Green is common in Indian sets with lavishly decorated versions of conventional European pieces. India also produced many magnificent ornamental sets with the figures mounted on elephants or riding in chariots. Sets made to European specifications were also made in large numbers in Burma.

European carving is generally inferior to Far Eastern workmanship, although sets made in Dieppe (the centre of the French ivory trade) can be outstanding. English manufacturers tended to stick to designs which could be produced almost entirely on a lathe. One exception was the firm of Hastilow, whose 19th-century pieces, often standing on distinctive fluted columns, are much sought after by collectors. Price guides relate to the sets, not the individual figures.

▼ *Twelve men from a Lund chess set dating from the mid-1820s. The firm of Lund were based in Fleet Street, London; they designed their own sets, although they sometimes commissioned Indian craftsmen to make them.*

PRICE GUIDE **6**

▲ *Delicately carved pieces, which have clearly been influenced by oriental designs, from an early 19th-century ivory chess set. It is quite likely that they were actually made in India, like many 'English'-style sets.*

PRICE GUIDE **8**

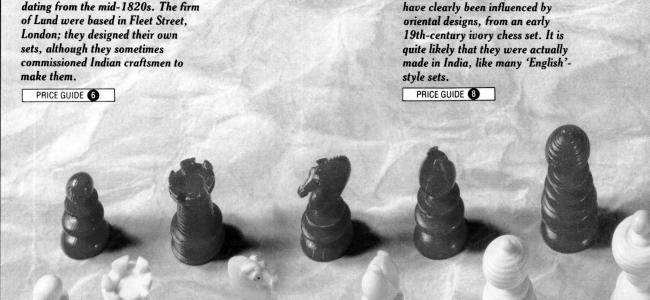

PRICE GUIDE ▶

COLLECTOR'S TIPS

There is no shortage of old chessmen; there must be hundreds of thousands scattered throughout the world, most of them of little value. On the other hand, some magnificent individual pieces are probably being used as ornaments, their owners unaware of the fact that they were originally chessmen.

Dating is notoriously difficult, even with some of the world's best-known chessmen. Estimates of the age of the famous Scandinavian walrus ivory pieces found on the Isle of Lewis in 1831 and now mainly in the British Museum have ranged from the 11th to the 17th century. It is unlikely that you will come across anything earlier than the late 18th century, but pinpointing a date of manufacture over the last two centuries can be just as difficult. Many wood and ivory designs were produced with little change, both in Europe and the Far East, throughout the 19th century and well into the 20th. Some of the most successful are still being produced, albeit in inferior materials and with inferior workmanship.

MAKERS' NAMES

With good-quality ivory sets from the last century, the maker's name is an invaluable guide. When it appears, which, unfortunately, is all too rarely, it is stamped on the base of the white king (and occasionally on the base of the red king as well). Names to look out for include William Lund, Toy Brothers, G. Merrifield and John Jaques. Boxed sets by these and other firms survive. The boxes range from plain, functional wooden ones to ornate papier-mâché caskets, with leather divisions or cotton or velvet linings to fit the pieces.

Chess Boards

MANY GEORGIAN CHESS SETS WOULD HAVE BEEN MADE WITH THEIR OWN BOARDS, BUT BOARDS AND PIECES HAVE OFTEN BEEN SEPARATED. BOARDS CAN BE ALMOST AS VARIED AS CHESSMEN; MOST WERE MADE OF HARDWOOD, AND GIVEN DECORATIVE INLAYS OF IVORY, MOTHER-OF-PEARL, BRASS, OR CONTRASTING-COLOURED WOODS, BUT FINELY WORKED LEATHER EXAMPLES WERE ALSO PRODUCED.

Cantonese Chess Set

TO CATER FOR GEORGIAN AND REGENCY TASTE FOR THE EXOTIC, THE EAST INDIA COMPANY IMPORTED A VAST NUMBER OF ORIENTAL GOODS, INCLUDING CHESS SETS PRODUCED IN CANTONESE WORKSHOPS. THE PIECES, WHICH WERE ALL CARVED FROM INDIAN IVORY, OFTEN REPRESENTED OPPOSING ORIENTAL ARMIES. THE SETS THAT WERE SPECIALLY PRODUCED FOR THE WEST FREQUENTLY PORTRAYED EUROPEAN RULERS ON THE WHITE SIDE; NAPOLEON AND JOSEPHINE AND THE ENGLISH GEORGES WERE PARTICULAR FAVOURITES, AND THEY WERE SHOWN OPPOSING CHINESE AND MANCHU EMPERORS AND EMPRESSES. RESERVING THE WHITE SIDE FOR THE EUROPEANS WAS A PIECE OF FLATTERY, SINCE THE PLAYER WITH THE WHITE PIECES HAS THE ADVANTAGE OF FIRST MOVE.

① THE WHITE KING REPRESENTS GEORGE III AND THE QUEEN IS HIS WIFE, QUEEN CHARLOTTE.

② THE QUALITY OF THE CARVING IS VERY HIGH; DETAILS OF DRESS ARE PRECISELY RENDERED.

③ OVAL BASES ARE A STANDARD FEATURE OF CANTONESE SETS; IN THE BEST EXAMPLES THE FIGURES AND BASES ARE CARVED FROM ONE PIECE OF IVORY.

④ ALTHOUGH THE KING, QUEEN AND BISHOP ON THE WHITE SIDE WEAR WESTERN DRESS, THE PAWNS DO NOT. THIS ONE BRANDISHES AN ORIENTAL SCIMITAR WHICH CAN BE REMOVED FROM HIS HAND.

·CLOSE UP·

① FLOWER-LIKE FORMS

② REALISM

③ LATHE TURNING

④ CAREFULLY OBSERVED DETAILS

① THE CARVING ON THIS PIECE RESEMBLES UNFOLDING PETALS.

② THE ROOK IN THIS SET IS MODELLED ON A CASTLE'S KEEP.

③ MANY IVORY CHESS PIECES WERE TURNED ON THE LATHE.

④ THE MANE WHICH FALLS TO ONE SIDE IS A WELL OBSERVED DETAIL.

⑤ THE VIGOUR OF THE REARING HORSE SHOWS IT WAS MODELLED BY A SCULPTOR.

⑥ INTRICATE CARVING SUCH AS THIS COULD ONLY HAVE BEEN DONE BY HAND.

⑤ EXCELLENT MODELLING

⑥ HAND CARVING

Most of the time, however, collectors and dealers are faced with incomplete sets, of which it is possible to say only that they were made some time in the last century. Unless they are of a strikingly unusual design, sets with the odd pawn and knight's head missing are best avoided. Better one complete set than three or four with pieces from other sets substituted for the originals. Inevitably, over the years sets have been made up from different sources. If someone has one set with, say, a rook missing and another similar set, incomplete but with all four rooks present, there is a strong temptation to cannibalize the one set to complete the other.

Since the number of complete old sets is limited, many enthusiasts find satisfying consolation in collecting odd individual pieces in as many styles as they can find. Naturally they tend to go for finely-carved major pieces in ivory, rather than a vast army of wooden pawns.

RECOGNIZING CRAFTSMANSHIP
Learning to recognize the quality of ivory carving is an essential requirement for any collector, especially one aiming to concentrate on Indian and Chinese chessmen. The quality of the craftsmanship can vary enormously between what appears, superficially, to be two indentical sets. It will also help you to spot any odd men out in hybrid chess sets. You should see and preferably handle as many Anglo-Indian sets as

possible, before plunging in and buying one from an antique shop. You may not know exactly how old it is, but you will know that you have a good one.

Although dealers may be a little optimistic in the dates they ascribe to their sets, they are unlikely to mislead you about the material they are made of. Nevertheless, you should acquaint yourself thoroughly with the different kinds of ivory, bone and horn, and modern plastic imitations. It is often difficult to tell bone from Indian ivory, which bleaches with age in rather the same way. Where the bone has dried out, there are tiny pits which will gradually gather dirt, but even experts are sometimes forced to use a magnifying glass to spot them. In this, as with all antique objects, there is no substitute for experience in handling the pieces.

Collectors, faced with the bewildering variety of chess sets produced over the last 200 years, may choose to restrict the field in which they operate. Some may decide to collect playing sets rather than decorative ones, but any lover of chess sets will, sooner or later, be attracted by an entertaining oddity, where the pieces are animals, opposing armies of political parties, or even abstract modernistic shapes. Chess sets undoubtedly have personalities; in a standard playing set it is immediately apparent in the expression on the faces of the knights. This is no accident: the horse's head is usually the one part of the set which has to

be carved rather than turned. A well-made knight is indicative of the quality of the whole set.

POINTS TO WATCH
■ Old boards are much rarer than old pieces. When a board is offered for sale with a set, there is often no connection between the two.

■ Porcelain and pottery designs, like the famous Wedgwood Flaxman set, have often been reproduced officially and unofficially.

■ Washing ivory or bone pieces in water can have disastrous results, particulary with stained pieces, because of the porous nature of the material.

■ Many bone (and some ivory) pieces are made in sections which screw together. Take great care when dismantling them.

■ New boxwood sets are expensive. It is possible to find late 19th- and early 20th-century sets for about the same price.

▶ *The popularity of chess in Georgian England is reflected in the number of porcelain groups showing chess players that were made at the time.*

The Edwardian Lobby

The country house lobby was the muddy boots entrance for the comings and goings of the family and contained everything they needed outdoors

The side lobby in Edwardian houses was plain and functional. This was in contrast to the front entrance which was designed to impress visitors and was enriched with oak panelling, oriental rugs, fine furniture, pictures and porcelain.

There was usually a plain tiled floor in the lobby because it was the muddy boots entrance, used by people coming back from the stables and the gardens and from country walks with the dogs in all weathers. It was the place to put on outdoor clothing before setting off in the pony and trap, and a place to store wellington boots, hats and garden games.

It is often difficult to find storage space for such things in modern homes, so a large back porch, utility room or garden room is often built on, very much in the style of the Edwardian lobby, with the same kind of furniture.

It can be a light and sunny place, ideal for green plants, and, as in the Edwardian lobby, all the summer sports equipment can be stored there.

An Edwardian lobby with a more contemporary look – and where the occupants obviously lead a less countryfied lifestyle.

these years seem to be bathed in perpetual sunshine.

Writers of the time have described the delicious odour of these country houses as a mixture of wood smoke, oil lamps, dogs and tobacco, with wafts of the country coming in the windows.

THE ROOM'S DECOR

The lobby entrance to the house was usually at the side, with an outer door of stout oak and inner double doors that could be set open with door stops. The outer door might have stained glass panels, but was generally of a plainer design than the front door.

The walls were often partly panelled or simply whitewashed or distempered. Dark holly green was a favoured colour, or dark brown. There would be large areas of glass, with windows on three sides and a conservatory-style glass roof, so it was a good place for plants. Banks of bright geraniums were very popular and there was always a plant stand or octagonal table for an aspidistra.

Hanging on the walls would be amateur water-colours of local scenes, crayon sketches by members of the family and perhaps a portrait of a favourite dog.

There might also be a display of stuffed mammals, gamebirds or fish. These were highly prized in Edwardian times. Subsequently they fell out of favour, but are now much sought-after by collectors.

The flooring of terracotta tiles or dark green linoleum was usually uncarpeted. Through the inner double doors the lobby connected with a passageway to the smoking room or billiard room. A baize swing door led to the back kitchen premises, and there was a nursery passageway where the perambulators were kept and another door to the front hall and staircase.

The lobby was simply furnished. A chair or two

Edwardian country houses were attractive, comfortable homes, owned not only by the local gentry but also by the new class of successful businessmen. Having made their fortunes, these entrepreneurs bought country houses so that they could feel a part of the establishment.

In the country there were all the pleasures of hunting, shooting and fishing, or of playing tennis, and visiting other county families. Friends would arrive for weekend house-parties by train and there would be country drives, picnics and garden parties to enjoy.

During this time there were all the exciting discoveries of cycling and the motor car, but the country lifestyle was slow to change. The Edwardian years, between the opening of the new century and the outbreak of war, were golden years for the well-to-do. The atmosphere was more relaxed and less censorious and straitlaced than in Victorian times. There were plenty of servants – a staff of about six in a country house of any size – and in popular memory

▲ Country houses generally had a full complement of guests at the weekend when friends were invited down from London. The more active would partake in country sports, a cricket match, croquet, badminton or tennis. Tea would often be taken on the lawn in summer.

▶ Today, the umbrella stand is still ideal for storing all the paraphernalia needed for country walks and sports. Stowed in this painted cast-iron stand are fishing gear and various sticks and brollies.

▼ *At a time when no city gent would be seen without a brolly, the umbrella was an essential part of everyone's wardrobe. Ladies carried more colourful ones.*

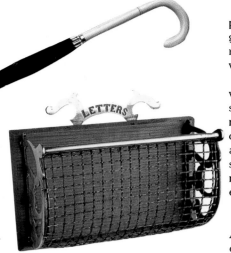

▶ *Outgoing post would be placed in the letter rack which was often situated in the lobby. One of the servants would take the mail to the post office.*

provided somewhere to sit when putting on boots or gaiters. They were usually plain country chairs, with rush seats. The servants would sit on them when waiting for family departures and arrivals.

There was always a table, perhaps of fine oak, which was plain with straight tapered legs and shallow drawers. In these drawers were kept the miscellaneous things that so often get mislaid – a clothes brush, gloves, prayerbooks, brown paper and string and a few simple tools such as a hammer, scissors and a tape measure in a leather case for marking out the tennis court. Maps and games equipment might also be kept in these drawers.

STORAGE SPACE

An important storage item in most lobbies was an oak chest. Beautifully carved, this might have been in the family for many generations and would have

---

LIFE AND LEISURE

Anyone for Tennis?

LAWN TENNIS FITTED SO WELL INTO THE OPEN-AIR LIVES OF THE ENGLISH MIDDLE CLASSES THAT IT BECAME UNIVERSALLY POPULAR. IT COULD BE PLAYED ON LAWNS OF MODERATE SIZE, AT NO GREAT EXPENSE. IT ALSO PROVIDED WOMEN WITH THEIR FIRST REAL CHANCE TO INDULGE IN SPORT.

THE ENCUMBERING CLOTHES WOMEN WORE ON THE TENNIS COURTS DID NOT PERMIT ANY STRENUOUS ACTION. IN THE EARLY DAYS THEY WORE LONG, TRAILING, BUSTLED SKIRTS, TIGHT CORSETS, BLOUSES WITH VOLUMINOUS SLEEVES, FLOWERY HATS AND SHOES WITH HIGH HEELS.

BY EDWARDIAN TIMES, LADIES PHOTOGRAPHED IN THEIR GARDENS 'READY FOR TENNIS' WORE ELABORATE LACE-COLLARED BLOUSES, LONG DARK SKIRTS AND BOATERS.

MRS FENWICK, WHO WON THE LADIES CHAMPIONSHIP IN 1908, WORE LONG WHITE SKIRTS WHICH WERE VERY FULL AND SWIRLING. IT WAS 1919 BEFORE SUZANNE LENGLEN SUCCEEDED IN ESTABLISHING SHORTER SKIRTS FOR TENNIS AND IT WAS NOT UNTIL 1931 THAT MRS FEARNLEY-WHITTINGSTALL ABANDONED CORSET AND SUSPENDER BELT AND APPEARED ON THE COURT WITH BARE LEGS. THAT, HOWEVER, WAS IN AMERICA.

▲ COUNTRY HOUSE TENNIS AROUND THE TURN OF THE CENTURY WAS A FASHIONABLE, SOCIAL EVENT AND A PLEASANT WAY TO UNDERTAKE SOME NONE TOO STRENUOUS EXERCISE. THE DICTATES OF FASHION AND PROPRIETY OBLIGED PLAYERS – WOMEN ESPECIALLY – TO WEAR CLOTHES THAT WERE GLAMOROUS BUT CONSTRICTING.

▶ ONE OF THE CHIEF ATTRACTIONS OF TENNIS WAS THAT IT ALLOWED YOUNG PEOPLE TO GET TOGETHER. IN THE EARLY DAYS, THEY STILL USUALLY PLAYED UNDER THE CHAPERONING EYES OF THEIR ELDERS.

▲ *In addition to regular social events, such as May Balls and Debs' Dances, the country house year revolved around highlights in the sporting calendar. This picture, 'The First of October', shows gentlemen taking a buffet luncheon on the first day of the pheasant shooting season. At such times the house would be full with an influx of visitors from town. Earlier in the year, houses near the moors of the north and west would host the guns for the Glorious Twelfth (August 12th) and the start of grouse shooting.*

The winter months would see visitors arriving for a weekend with the hunt. Come spring and summer, gentlemen in their tweeds would arrive with their rods for the early salmon run or the opening of the trout fishing season.

▶ *The boot rack was a convenient way to store footwear. Wet and muddy boots could be hung up on entering the lobby. This ornate Victorian boot rack is made of mahogany.*

mellowed to a really attractive warm glowing colour.

In these chests Edwardian families stored tennis rackets in their presses, Slazenger tennis balls, maybe a cricket bat, croquet mallets and golf clubs, as well as dog leads and collars, skipping ropes, hoops, ice skates and roller skates.

There would certainly be a cupboard for coats in the lobby, with a ledge above for men's hats. Hall cupboards were sometimes very fine oak wardrobes that had been relegated to the back premises when mahogany bedroom furniture became the fashion. Some marvellous discoveries have been made when the layers of paint have been stripped away from these cupboards and medieval oak carving revealed.

In the cupboards would hang the overcoats and mackintoshes in everyday use. There would be thick tweed coats for winter walks, fur-lined coats for driving in open vehicles and lightweight ones to keep off the dust of the unmetalled roads in summer.

On the hat shelf were bowlers, soft felts and cloth caps for everyday use, panama hats for summer and motoring veils when the first cars came into use. Top hats might be kept there in their boxes. They were not used so frequently in Edwardian times, but were essential for weddings, funerals and special events, and were not always black but sometimes grey. Opera top hats with their long silk pile and stout hunting hats could both be washed in soap and water and smoothed with a special curved iron.

The bottom of the cupboard housed leather boots, galoshes that were put on over ordinary shoes and rubber wellington boots that superseded them about this time. Leather gaiters with tiny button fastenings were also kept in this cupboard.

An umbrella stand, divided into sections by brass rails and fitted with a drip tray, was a necessity in the lobby. This held leather-seated and cane-seated shooting sticks as well as slim umbrellas. The best

gilt-handled, initialled umbrellas came from Briggs. There would also be a variety of stout walking sticks — ash staves for everyday use and older ones with elaborate horn handles.

ODDS AND ENDS

On the wall there would be a rack for hunting-crops. These had cane or leather-covered stocks about 15 inches (37 cm) long, with a roughened horn crook at one end for opening gates.

A bootscraper always stood just outside the lobby

▲ *As well as a wardrobe for outdoor gear, the lobby would have coat hooks for damp overcoats, caps and mufflers. These hooks are of china and brass.*

door. Some houses had an additional bootscraper inside the lobby, fitted with brushes and a coconut mat, to ensure that little mud entered the house.

There would be a plain mirror in a walnut frame over the table. This was important for checking the set of one's hat at a time when hats were worn universally.

If there was no gun-room in the house, then the gun cupboard might be in the lobby and would always be locked. The game-carrier might also be stored here. This useful piece of equipment was made of wooden slats with a leather handle and brass fittings, designed so that a number of gamebirds could be hung from it and carried home.

The gong which summoned the household to meals was usually on the main staircase but was sometimes found in the lobby. One of the servants would beat a tattoo on it with a chamois-leather covered drumstick. Siegfried Sassoon describes in his autobiography how the gong 'boomed obsequiously' in the Mayfair house of his grand relations, but had a jolly 'it's-your-own-fault-if-you're-late' sound at his boyhood country home in Kent.

THE OUTDOOR LIFE

With all the chores done for them, the family had leisure to enjoy the outdoor life to the full. Sports and games were very popular with large Edwardian

families. They played golf on a nearby course and cricket on the village green. When they wanted to ride, the groom would saddle the horse. If a picnic was planned, the hampers would be well packed with rich fare and a servant would be on hand to lay the picnic cloth.

The image that endures from these leisured times is of tea tables set out on shady green lawns with gracious hostesses pouring tea from silver teapots.

▲ *In a busy household the lobby would soon become cluttered as the family and their guests discarded footwear and coats on their return from an outing. It would fall to the servants to see that everything was cleaned.*

LIFE AND LEISURE

Mackintoshes and Burberries

RAINCOATS ARE ESSENTIAL FOR AN ACTIVE OUTDOOR LIFE IN THE COUNTRY. IN EDWARDIAN TIMES, MACKINTOSHES WERE MADE FROM AN INDIA RUBBER CLOTH WHICH HAD BEEN PATENTED IN 1836.

BURBERRIES WERE INVENTED BY THE FIRM OF THAT NAME. THEIR COATS FOR MEN AND WOMEN STOOD UP WELL TO HARD USE. MADE OF A GREENISH BROWN MATERIAL, LINED EITHER WITH SHOT SILK OR CHECKED WOOL, THEY HUNG LOOSELY FROM THE SHOULDERS WITHOUT A BELT. BUTTONED TABS COULD BE FASTENED HIGH AROUND THE THROAT IN A DOWNPOUR AND THE CUFFS COULD BE TIGHTENED TO KEEP OUT THE DRIPS. THE POCKETS WERE IN THE LINING AND WERE REACHED THROUGH SLITS, SO MOST THINGS KEPT DRY IN THEM.

▼ BURBERRY'S PRODUCED A RANGE OF WEATHERPROOF TOP-COATS FOR ALL TOWN AND COUNTRY PURSUITS.

▲ A WOOLLEN BURBERRY WITH A QUILTED LINING WAS IDEAL WHEN DRIVING A PONY AND TRAP.

The Cricket Bat

The Edwardian era can truly be described as a golden age for British cricket, producing many superb players and a wealth of cricketing equipment and ephemera

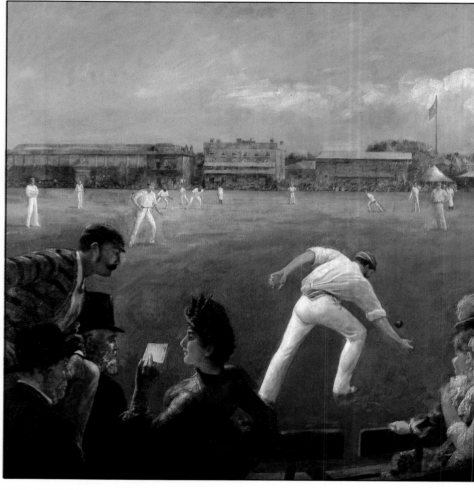

Few Edwardian schoolboys would have been without sporting heroes or sporting mementoes, for this was an age in which Britain was the champion on the playing fields, just as conclusively as she was the dominant voice in world affairs. The King himself, although not an athlete, was a 'sporting monarch', devoted to horse-racing and yachting, and the all-round athletic prowess of the country can be gauged from the results of the 1908 Olympic Games, held in London. Britain came first by winning 56 events, the United States was second with 22 wins and the third nation – Sweden – trailed far behind with a mere eight.

The pattern was similar elsewhere. At Wimbledon, one or other of the two Doherty brothers won the men's singles every year, except one, between 1897 and their retirement in 1906, and they regularly won the doubles together. In football the English team beat a German side 12-0 and 10-1 in 1901, and British performers regularly carried off the top prizes in rowing, golf and other sports.

AMATEURISM

The middle-class schoolboy could readily identify with his heroes, for although some top sportsmen were professionals, the majority were still amateurs and, therefore, 'gentlemen'. Versatility, suggesting easy mastery rather than specialized training, was the order of the day, the most astonishing exemplar being C. B. Fry. He was one of the greatest cricketers of all time whose feat of scoring centuries in six successive innings has never been surpassed. He was also a football international, a fine rugby player and boxer, and a world-class athlete.

Cricketing Memorabilia

THE GAME OF CRICKET HAS GIVEN RISE TO A LARGE SOUVENIR INDUSTRY. APART FROM THE EQUIPMENT AND DRESS USED IN THE ACTUAL GAME, THE COLLECTOR CAN CHOOSE FROM A VAST ARRAY OF CRICKETING MEMORABILIA IN SILVER, PORCELAIN, POTTERY AND METAL. PHOTOGRAPHS AND PRINTED EPHEMERA – LIKE CARTOONS, CIGARETTE CARDS SHOWING FAMOUS PLAYERS, AND COPIES OF WISDEN'S ALMANACK – ARE HIGHLY SOUGHT AFTER, AS ARE UNUSUAL ITEMS SUCH AS CRICKET BALL CIGARETTE LIGHTERS.

In 1892, as a Classics scholar at Oxford University (where he had been placed first in his scholarship examination), he took part in a match against Cambridge; putting down his cigar, he equalled the world long-jump record, then casually finished his smoke. He was reckoned to have the physique and features of a Greek god, and was a figure of such natural authority that legend had it that the Albanians considered offering him their throne. Small wonder he was idolized.

As an all-round athlete, Fry was peerless, but in cricket he was matched and even surpassed by some of his contemporaries, for the Edwardian period was, by any standards, the golden age of the game. W. G. Grace, who dominated cricket to an extent that no one else has ever dominated any other game, was probably the most popular and easily recognized man in the country. He had virtually retired by 1906, but in his wake came superlative players, such as Ranjitsinhji and Jack Hobbs. Pitches had improved greatly since Grace began his career, and although there was no shortage of fine bowlers, the bat generally dominated the ball and the heavy scoring made for entertaining play. Consequently, cricket was followed by huge numbers of people, either in the flesh or in lengthy newspaper reports.

The familiar organization of English cricket into county sides took shape in the 1860s and 1870s, but the origins of the game are much older. Its early history is obscure, but a form of the game existed in the Middle Ages perhaps as early as 1300, where

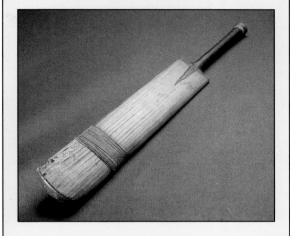

A TYPICAL EDWARDIAN CRICKET BAT WITH A TWINE-COVERED HANDLE. OTHER TYPES OF HANDLE INCLUDED THE 'ALL CANE' VARIETY AND THOSE COVERED IN INDIA RUBBER.

▲ By the 1880s Test Matches between England and Australia were a regular feature of the British way of life. This painting captures a specific moment in the 1886 Lord's Test: the Australian T. W. Garrett is about to field the ball bowled by Fred Spofforth and hit by W. G. Grace. But some people in the audience seem strangely unaffected by the cricketing drama: in the foreground to the right of the stand the beautiful Lily Langtry – rumoured to be the mistress of the future Edward VII – turns away as the Prince and Princess of Wales approach from the right.

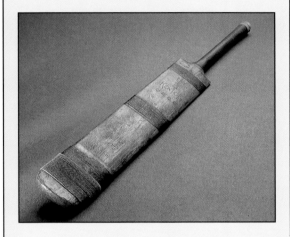

THIS EDWARDIAN BAT HAS SUFFERED EXTENSIVE DAMAGE TO THE BLADE – SEVERAL LENGTHS OF TWINE HAVE BEEN USED TO BIND THE SPLIT WOOD TOGETHER.

there is a reference in a royal account to the future Edward II (then aged 16) playing a game called 'creag'. By the 17th century there were organized clubs and prestige matches, sometimes for large wagers. The Marylebone Cricket Club (MCC), the game's governing body, was founded in 1787, and the first international contest took place in 1859, when an English team visited Canada and the USA. The first recognized Test Match, between England and Australia, was played in Melbourne in 1877.

A SCHOOLBOY'S SPORT

Cricket was being taken seriously by schools by the 18th century, and by Edwardian times it formed part of every schoolboy's curriculum. In fact, some public schools took the sport so seriously that they employed former county professionals as coaches.

Boys were brought up to play cricket not just because it was healthy exercise, but also because it was considered character-building. The boy who conducted himself well on the field, so the idea ran, would grow into a mature, honourable man. This

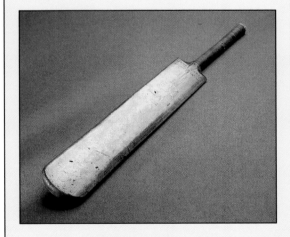

A POLISHED BAT IN REASONABLE CONDITION. IT IS SLIGHTLY SMALLER THAN A CONVENTIONAL ADULT BAT AS IT WAS SPECIALLY MADE FOR A YOUNGER PLAYER.

idea of cricket as a metaphor of life has resulted in many cricketing expressions entering everyday language: 'batting on a sticky wicket', 'playing with a straight bat' and, of course, 'it's not cricket'.

CRICKET BAT DESIGN

Not all players have had high sporting ideals, however. In 1771 a player called 'Shock' White, from Reigate, went out to play with a bat that was wider than the wicket, so the laws of the game were amended to specify a maximum width of 4¼ inches (11cm). This has remained unchanged right up to the present day.

The maximum length of a full-size bat is 38 inches (95cm), but the proportion of handle to bat can vary considerably, some batsmen preferring a long handle, others a short one. This, like the weight of the bat (on which there is no restriction), remains a matter of personal preference. There are also smaller-sized bats made for children.

The main area of change has been in the shape of the bat. The earliest bats were essentially long, heavy clubs which curved outwards towards the bottom. This shape reflected the prevalent conditions and style of play: underarm bowling and unscientific slogging. As the game grew in finesse, however, the bat evolved to its present well-balanced and standardized shape and size.

Until about the middle of the 19th century, cricket bats were made all in one piece, but then the sprung handle was introduced, acting as a shock absorber. This was the last major stage in the cricket bat's evolution, and the bats used by W. G. Grace were, in all essentials, the same as those used today. The now familiar rubber covering of the twine binding of the handle was introduced towards the end of Grace's career, but some batsmen, notably the great Australian Victor Trumper, preferred the feel of the bat without it.

Major manufacturers, such as Crawford, Gun and Moore, Gray-Nicholls, and Warsop, some of whom are still in business today, made their bats from East Anglian willow, which combined lightness with durability and springiness. Around 1898 a top quality bat from a reputable store would have cost about 25 shillings (£1.25).

CRICKETING BYGONES

The Edwardian schoolboy lavished time and attention on caring for his cricket bat, as articles in the *Boy's Own Paper* of that time testify. Advice on washing, oiling, and sanding and storing were

---

·PRICE GUIDE· CRICKET EQUIPMENT

Second-hand cricketing equipment and clothing is usually well within the price range of most sports enthusiasts. Bats, stumps, blazers and caps are relatively plentiful and inexpensive, and there are now a few specialists who deal in this field. Depending on the celebrity of the player or players, signed bats can fetch several hundred pounds.

▼ *Two boldly striped blazers, which would help the aspiring sportsman to cut a dash at the cricket club. One has a beautifully embroidered badge on the breast pocket.*

PRICE GUIDE ❹

▼ *A charming sepia photograph dated 1904, showing a group of amateur players at Oakfield Cricket Club, splendidly kitted out in whites, blazers and caps.*

PRICE GUIDE ❹

▼▸ *Two cricket caps. One is cloth with a removable metal badge; the other is velvet with embroidery.*

PRICE GUIDE ❷

▼▼ *A set of stumps with brass tops, in excellent condition. The bails which should sit on top during the game appear to be missing.*

PRICE GUIDE ❹

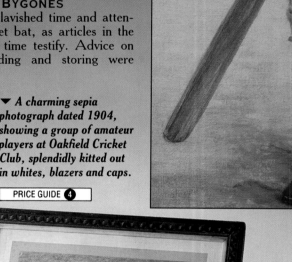

enthusiastically reported and could well account for some of the fine examples that occasionally turn up in antique shops today.

However, the value and collectability of a bat depend largely on its associations. Signed bats are reasonably commonplace, but the status of a player, or the importance of the event commemorated, are generally much more important than the bat's condition (although a well-cared-for example will obviously be more desirable than one that is falling apart).

The same principles generally apply to other items of cricketing memorabilia: clothing, such as international caps or blazers; trophies (where the value also depends on their precious metal content); souvenir programmes; photographs of players, teams or matches; novelty items, such as cigarette cards; and, not least, books.

Cricket has by far the richest literature of any sport, and several booksellers specialize in it. Most famous players have committed themselves to print at some time (often in ghosted autobiographies), and *Wisden's Cricketers' Almanack*, first published in 1864, is the most famous yearbook in sport. Complete sets are much sought after, but rarely come on the market; even single volumes, particularly of early years, can be valuable.

It is only fairly recently that sporting memorabilia has become established as an important specialist field in the antiques world. Few shops or dealers specialize in it yet, but the major auction houses now hold sales fairly regularly, and in 1987 there was an important auction at Lord's Cricket Ground to celebrate the bicentenary of the MCC. Some of the prices fetched here exceeded all expectations, but this probably reflects the unique nature of the occasion, rather than suggesting a sudden price inflation in cricketing bygones.

▲ *An Edwardian mahogany stand lined with green baize, used for storing cricket bats and balls.*

PRICE GUIDE ⑤

▲ *The distinctive black-bearded figure of W. G. Grace, the dominant personality in British cricket at the turn of the century.*

◀▼ *A complete set of Wisden's cricket balls with their presentation box. Balls sold in sets like this will be slightly more expensive than those sold singly.*

PRICE GUIDE ③

▼ *Two straw boaters. During the Edwardian era, as now, boaters were worn by spectators rather than players – they shielded the eyes from the sun on hot summer afternoons.*

PRICE GUIDE ③

▼ *A pair of cricket pads in fair condition, although a little worn. Their leather straps are still intact.*

PRICE GUIDE ②

▼▼ *Two Edwardian cricket bats in reasonable, but not perfect, condition. The one underneath shows signs of repair to the blade.*

PRICE GUIDE ③

Motoring and Cycling Costume

The Edwardian motorist in his grotesque goggles and voluminous coat was the butt of mockery; the knickerbockered cyclist, however, was considered sensibly dressed for outdoor pursuits

Wealthy Edwardians spent much of their daily routine getting in and out of various sets of clothes: ladies changed from walking dress to riding habit and from tea-gown to evening dress, while the gentlemen exchanged hunting or shooting clothes for lounge suit or tails. When it became clear that a whole new costume was needed to indulge in the new fashion for motoring, they accepted this as another inevitable fact of life.

Special protective clothing was essential because the earliest cars were open vehicles on which driver and passengers sat high above the road, exposed to the elements and, since there were at first no windscreens, all the mud, dust and stone chippings

▼ *This cycling costume, worn by a chic lady cyclist in 1896, was somewhat daring for the time. Without the encumbrances of heavy motoring gear – goggles, cloak and cap – she was free to don a jaunty straw boater, a pair of practical bloomers, perhaps under a long skirt if she was more modest and a fashionable high-buttoned blouse before setting off.*

were forcibly thrown up from the untarred roads.

The names that were given to models of motor car around the turn of the century – such as 'wagonette', 'landaulette' and 'voiturette', show that they were still conceived as horseless versions of traditional horse-drawn vehicles. The coachwork, such as it was, was built by the same firms that provided the coachwork for horse-drawn carriages. In the 1890s most English people thought of motoring as a hobby for hardy eccentrics rather than a convenient way to travel. In the early years of this century, the motoring lobby grew and, as a result of the Motor Car Act which came into force on January 1st 1904, the speed limit was raised from 14 to 20 m.p.h., cars were registered for the first time and car-owners were required to obtain a licence (although drivers did not have to take a test until 1934). Up to this point the British had rather lagged behind the French and Germans in the development of the motor car: as late as 1896 cars were obliged by law to travel at no more than 4 m.p.h., preceded by a man with a red flag.

UNATTRACTIVE ATTIRE

Pioneering motorists of the 1890s had given little thought to the elegance of their appearance. Their prime concern was to protect the eyes from flying stones and horse-shoe nails, and, in the summer, from clouds of dust. To do this they donned goggles very similar to those used by workmen engaged in dangerous occupations, such as the stone-breaking gangs who built the roads they travelled on.

In the most widely-used style of motoring goggles, the convex eye-glasses were held in nickel or aluminium rims. For a snug fit, the silk frames were edged with chenille and the goggles were held in place with an elastic band fastened at the back of the head. But there were countless variations on this basic style. Some motorists liked to attach their goggles like spectacles with wire ear-pieces, many chose rubber or leather instead of silk and a few, who found goggles too restricting, wore one-piece masks or eye-shields made of mica. There were also versions with glass at the sides to increase the wearer's field of vision. Most makers offered a choice of clear or tinted glasses and some even sold masks (normally used for racing) which shielded the whole face from wind, rain, grit and dust.

As they were all too conscious of the possibility that they would have to descend from the car to make some mechanical adjustments or to change a tyre (the wheels on the earliest cars were not detachable), these driver/mechanics dressed roughly, wearing high-buttoned reefer jackets, leather waistcoats for extra warmth and breeches and leather leggings rather than trousers. Their favoured headgear was a soft peaked cap with flaps that could be brought down over the ears. In winter they needed long overcoats that could be wrapped around the legs to keep out the wind.

A FASHIONABLE PASTIME

As motoring gradually became fashionable in the early years of this century, the 'dirty work' was increasingly performed by a skilled chauffeur. This allowed passengers to devote more time and money to their clothes, and tailors and outfitters started to produce a new range of elegant motoring attire. The most expensive item in a gentleman motorist's wardrobe was his winter overcoat. The basic model was a full-length, double-breasted ulster of woollen cloth with a fur lining. Every imaginable rodent, marsupial and cat was used by the fur trade in Edwardian times, from hamsters to wombats. Squirrel skins, imported in vast numbers from Russia and Germany, were a very popular lining for men's motoring coats, but they were not as warm or as durable as the more expensive musquash and beaver.

Sealskin caps and coats were eminently practical because they could be washed, but the Englishman preferred not to have fur or skin on the outside of his coat; it made him look like the more flashy Continental motorists, who drove around ostentatiously in wolf- or foal-skin coats.

Leather coats had an unmistakable dash and were worn by some Englishmen who wanted to show off at the wheel, but good taste prescribed a coat of sober greyish tweed or Irish frieze. The now-celebrated firms of Burberry's and Aquascutum struck just the right note with their waterproofed motoring coats. Burberry's 'Viator' and 'Rusitor' (motorist's Latin for 'a man who goes to the country') were popular models for the well-dressed winter motorist.

DUST-PROOF CLOTHING

In summer a very different garment was needed in order to deal with the problem of dust. Loose fitting, light dust coats made of alpaca, silk or holland became almost as much a trademark of the motorist as their goggles. White dust coats were very dashing, but grey and fawn were rather more practical colours, as they did not show the accumulation of dirt so quickly. Unfortunately pedestrians at the roadside often suffered more from the dust than the well-protected motorist. Dust coats, like winter motoring

▲ *A French illustration of a group of women and children motorists in 1909. Their enveloping heavy fur coats, particularly popular on the Continent, or more elegant tweed coats, teamed with bizarre headgear, explain perfectly why motorists were mocked for their appearance. Women's hoods had to fulfil several functions: they protected women from the elements, as well as accommodating their elaborate hairstyles and hats. Women tended to reject goggles as being far too unattractive, although one woman can be seen wearing them. Motoring outfits for children were similar to adults' – scaled-down fur coats, hats and goggles.*

Motoring Caps & Helmets

A SNUG RACING HELMET WITH FLEECY LINING AND PROTECTIVE FLAP WHICH SECURES UNDER THE CHIN. WORN WITH GOGGLES, BOTH WERE MADE c. 1920.

A WOOLLEN BALACLAVA, WORN EITHER COVERING ALL BUT THE EYES, OR ROLLED UP OVER THE PEAK. IT WAS MADE c. 1930.

THIS MOTORING CAP c. 1910, WITH STRAPS WHICH COULD BE FASTENED UNDER THE CHIN, WAS ONE OF THE MORE COMMON STYLES FOR MEN.

becoming bow under the chin. When the dust became insufferable, it was pulled over the face.

Such veils were fine for informal visiting or summer excursions in the countryside, but if women were being driven in the car when going out to a formal occasion — a dinner or a ball — the protection they offered was insufficient. If she was sporting a magnificent hair-do and a dressy hat, a woman sometimes had to have recourse to a motoring hood. The most fantastic of these, built on a rigid wire frame covered with veiling, had a futuristic-looking window made of mica.

The typical car of the late Edwardian period was the long open tourer, normally used only in summer, in which the passengers could be sheltered by a hood, although the chauffeur in front remained exposed to the elements, like the coachman of old. The limousine with its high solid coachwork, in which the chauffeur was also protected (at least by a roof and a windscreen), was used for delivering passengers around town. The chauffeur's livery became very quickly standardized. Their familiar high-buttoned double-breasted tunic worn with matching breeches, boots and leggings was similar to the costume sported by many Edwardian motorcyclists. In bad weather they would wear a long, small-collared overcoat in exactly the same style as the tunic. The large leather gauntlets worn by all well-turned-out chauffeurs had been adopted at first to stop the wind getting up the sleeves of a driver's overcoat. When they became indelibly associated in people's minds with chauffeur's uniforms, motorists who drove their own cars took to wearing simpler tan gloves: it would never do to be mistaken for a chauffeur.

THE ESTABLISHED CYCLIST

Cyclists had, of course, been using Britain's roads rather longer than motorists. What had been a popular pursuit in the 1880s and a fashionable one among the upper and upper-middle classes in the 1890s, was, by the turn of the century, accepted by everybody as a normal method of travel. Working men now cycled to and from their jobs wearing their ordinary clothes, their trousers fastened with bicycle clips, but middle-class cyclists would dress up properly for a ride in the country, in a suit consisting

coats, usually had sleeves that could be sealed with an elasticated inner cuff or by means of straps.

For women, apart from the few adventurous spirits who drove their own cars and accepted it as an occupational hazard, dust was something of a nightmare. When motoring over to pay a visit in the summer, how was a woman to keep her clothes, hat, face and hair clean, so that she would be presentable on arrival? Long, full-skirted motoring coats on the same lines as men's, furs in winter, dust coats or light waterproof gaberdines in summer, solved the problem of her clothes, but her face and hair required more ingenious means of protection. Goggles and masks were made for women, but very few were prepared to disfigure themselves so hideously in public. The happiest solution was the combination of wide-brimmed hat and gauze veil. The veil, which might also be made of crêpe de chine, was at least two yards long, passing over the hat and tying in a

▲ All types of motoring and cycling clothing can be seen in this French poster. Hoods, helmets, goggles and bulky overcoats vie with sensible cyclists' knickerbockers and a cap.

◄▼ A pair of men's tweed knickerbockers, made around 1910, with ties below the knees.

PRICE GUIDE **4**

▼ A dark blue chauffeur's tunic with a double row of buttons and flap pockets, made around 1920.

PRICE GUIDE **5**

►▼ This pair of women's cycling bloomers, made c.1890, has a remarkably modern appeal.

PRICE GUIDE **5**

·*PRICE GUIDE*·〉 **CLOTHING**

Motoring and cycling clothing can still be found at reasonable prices. These will vary according to the condition and rarity of each item.

▼ A man's duster coat, made around 1900 in lightweight material to protect his clothes from the summer dust.

PRICE GUIDE **5**

▼ A detachable collar and panelled, front-patterned shirt, made around 1905.

PRICE GUIDE **4**

▼ This patterned silk bow tie, in a tan colour, was made around 1890.

PRICE GUIDE **3**

▼ A tweed sports jacket, made c.1908, with vertical and horizontal stripes.

PRICE GUIDE **6**

▼ This woollen waistcoat with checked design was made around 1900.

PRICE GUIDE **4**

of Norfolk jacket and knickerbockers, thick woollen socks, flat-heeled shoes, a flannel shirt with collar and tie, and a cloth cap.

In the 1890s daring women had appeared in 'rationals', or knickerbockers, in order to ride bicycles in greater comfort, but moral outrage was so violent, that few persevered with the fashion. It was however quite common to wear woollen knickerbockers under a long skirt while cycling. Skirts, usually of a plain-coloured serge, were adapted in various ways for cycling, some being cut specially to allow the skirt to hang down on either side of the back wheel, others weighted with lead to prevent the shameful exposure of a lady's legs. In colder weather women cyclists often wore a bodice cut in a style very similar to men's Norfolk jackets, but in summer they were more fortunate than men, being permitted to cycle in a high-buttoned blouse.

RACING CYCLISTS

Edwardian cyclists of both sexes dressed very much as people dressed for a wide range of outdoor pursuits, including walking, shooting, fishing and boating. Only racing cyclists were ever seen in shorts. The cyclists of the 1880s, many of whom belonged to cycling clubs, had been a far more spectacular sight, perched high on their 'ordinaries' or riding solid-tyred tricycles, and clothed in military-style patrol jackets with deerstalker or pill-box hats on their heads. After the pneumatic tyre was fitted to safety bicycles in 1888, the sport became much more comfortable, safer and more socially acceptable. In the early years of the century, cyclists joined with conservative pedestrians and equestrians in trying to stem the advance of the monstrously-attired 'Mr Toads', who terrorized other road-users with their new-fangled motor cars.

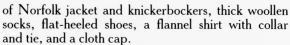

SMART HOODS AND VEILS

SHOWING VEIL UP.   SHOWING VEIL DOWN.

THE "BUCKINGHAM" HOOD.

Write for New Book "Creations for Ladies," showing the latest Motoring Modes.

THE "DAGMAR" HOOD.   "PRINCESS" VEIL.

ALFRED DUNHILL LIMITED
2, Conduit Street, Regent Street, London, W.
also at MANCHESTER and EDINBURGH.

▲ Ladies' motoring hoods were a futuristic blend of lace and mica to protect the face from dirt and draughts.

▲▶ A plain cream silk scarf with dark fringes. It has a monogrammed initial at one end.

PRICE GUIDE **3**

▶ A pair of men's leather leggings, made around 1920.

PRICE GUIDE **3**

▶ This pair of men's leather lace-up boots are in perfect condition.

PRICE GUIDE **5**

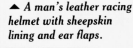

▲ A man's leather racing helmet with sheepskin lining and ear flaps.

PRICE GUIDE **3**

▼ A pair of leather motorcycling gauntlets, made around 1930.

PRICE GUIDE **4**

Motoring Memorabilia

From mascots and badges to posters, advertisements and magazines, the
collecting of motoring memorabilia is one of the fastest growing hobbies
today – with motoring enthusiasts of all ages

The collecting of motoring memorabilia, or automobilia, has become increasingly popular over the years. Collectors are interested in a very wide range of objects, in fact pretty well anything associated with motor cars or motorcycles other than the vehicles themselves. This includes motoring books and magazines, sales brochures, photographs, catalogues and competition programmes, as well as mascots, badges, radiator caps and lighting equipment.

The international combustion engine celebrated its 100th birthday in 1985, so some of the earliest automobilia may now be categorized as antiques even within the old, narrow definition of something over 100 years old. But all items from the period prior to the First World War have something of a classic status for the enthusiastic collector today.

MOTORING BOOKS

Technical books were not particularly popular with the Victorian and Edwardian motorist. He preferred travel logs and general interest books which captured some of the feelings of adventure and romance that motoring retained in those early days. Books like *Through Persia in a Motor Car* by Claude Anet, which appeared in 1907, were extremely popular. This described a journey from Bucharest to Constantinople by ten people in a 40HP Mercedes, a 20HP Mercedes and a 16HP Fiat, while *Pekin to Paris* by Luigi Barzini, first published in the same year, told the still more

GB Plate

THIS METAL PRE-1914 G B PLATE
WOULD HAVE BEEN ATTACHED TO THE
CAR BEFORE SETTING OFF ON A
MOTORING HOLIDAY ABROAD.

▶ *When the motor car was still a rare sight on the roads, going for a drive was such a special occasion that people often recorded the event on postcards, made from photographs.*

▼ *Motoring memorabilia encompasses a vast range of items including petrol cans, maps, goggles and gloves. In fact anything that is associated with the motor vehicle from its earliest days to the present can form part of a collection.*

romantic story of Prince Borghese's race across two continents in an Itala motor car.

These dramatic accounts appealed greatly to the early motorist struggling along the indifferent roads of Britain in vehicles which were still extremely unreliable, and remain of great historical interest to the modern collector. First editions are, of course, most collectable.

MAGAZINES

Around 1910 the motoring craze was booming, and magazines like *Motoring Illustrated* and *The Car Illustrated* began to appear. These were often sent to the publishers to be bound every half year, but unfortunately covers and advertisements were often discarded at this time. Bound collections of magazines are particularly collectable if they retain their covers and advertisements. Indeed these can be worth more than twice as much as those that are not intact.

Most of these early advertisements were fairly straightforward, often with quite detailed pictures of the vehicles. It was not until the 1920s that advertising copywriting really got into its stride. But one particularly famous creation of the marketing moguls dates from as early as 1898, when Michelin Man was born in Lyons. He appeared on posters that were lithographically reproduced, and often signed.

POSTERS

Some collectors specialize in early posters, concentrating on an individual make of car or a petrol company, or on one of the more famous graphic artists of the day such as Garry, Montaut, Géri or René Vincent. High quality re-issues of the work of these early French poster artists have been made, which are much cheaper than original prints.

LIGHTS

Because of the unreliability of their vehicles, motorists rarely ventured out on to the roads at night before 1900. In fact candle-powered carriage lamps fixed to these first cars were only intended as an aid to getting the vehicle home after dark in the event of a breakdown. But as reliability of cars improved, and lighting systems became more efficient, night-time driving became more common.

At this time lighting was not obligatory or standardized in any way, so there are many interesting variations in the equipment from the early days of motoring, making it one of the most popular areas for collectors of accessories. There were a variety of fuel systems used in these early lamps, including candle-power, oil, acetylene gas and, from the turn of the century, electricity.

MASCOTS AND BADGES

The pioneering motorist took great delight in personalizing his vehicle by attaching various kinds of mascots to it from soft toys to brass ornaments. It was not long before manufacturers began to produce mascots specifically designed for cars, and from about 1905 some well-designed models such as Rolls-Royce's 'Spirit of Ecstasy' were made, as well as a good deal of junk, much of which was sold by mail order.

The Automobile Club was founded in 1897 by F. R. Simms, becoming the Royal Automobile Club in 1907, when Edward VII agreed to become its patron. The RAC produced badges which were attached to the car, as did the Automobile Association founded in 1906. These, and various other kinds of badges, are usually grouped with mascots as an area for collecting, and can produce an extremely effective display.

Other items of possible interest to the collector of automobilia include models of early cars, motoring clothes, picnic sets, oil cans, petrol pump globes and dashboard instruments like speedometers, clocks and horns. Some collectors choose to specialize in a relatively narrow area – books and magazines perhaps – while others prefer to build up as wide a collection as possible, evoking every aspect of the excitement of these early days of motoring.

Printed Memorabilia

The first bound books about cars appeared in 1896. Knight's *Notes on Motor Carriages* and Lockert's *Les Voitures à Pétrole* are both highly prized collector's items today, and even copies which are not in very good condition fetch very high prices. Other early motoring books may be found with embossed covers and coloured motoring scenes on the front cover.

Sales catalogues and brochures are universally popular and quite common automobilia. Catalogues show the full range of a manufacturer's products with pictures and some technical detail, while sales brochures deal with just one model, and contain lots of glossy illustrations.

Before 1914 it was quite common for printed postcards to be ordered by individuals or by local clubs with photographs of a car and its owner or a club outing. These, as well as ordinary black and white photographs of the period, can be of considerable historical interest.

In 1895 *The Autocar* was published. It was the first British weekly motoring magazine, which was soon followed by many other magazines. The advertisements they contained, as well as car advertisements which appeared in general interest magazines, are of particular interest to the collector.

Posters, prints and pictures also form part of many collections of motoring memorabilia, as do competition programmes like the Brookland 'Official Race Cards'.

▶ *An intact and well-preserved magazine such as the July 1919 issue of* The Motor Owner *is very collectable. In this issue an advertisement for a car known as a King Eight Sporting Speedster faces an article on motoring in France.*

PRICE GUIDE ❸

▶ *The colourful front cover of the August 1919 edition of* The Motor Owner *no doubt inspired many motorists to drive to the seaside for the day.*

PRICE GUIDE ❸

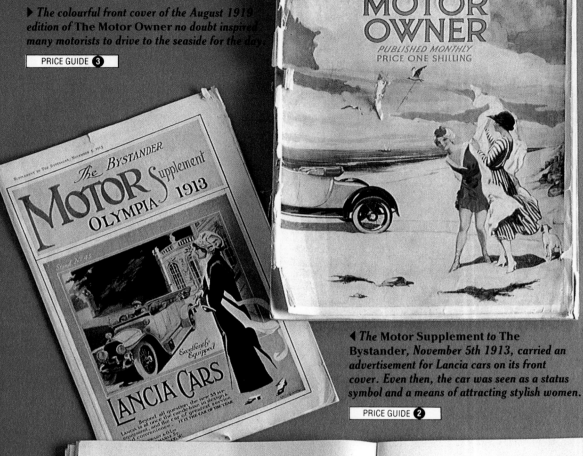

◀ *The* Motor Supplement *to* The Bystander, *November 5th 1913, carried an advertisement for Lancia cars on its front cover. Even then, the car was seen as a status symbol and a means of attracting stylish women.*

PRICE GUIDE ❷

PRICE GUIDE

◀ *It was not only the latest cars which were advertised in the motoring magazines. A colourful, sunlit scene is used here to promote Pratts petrol.*

PRICE GUIDE **2**

▼ *A romantic colour advertisement for Rolls-Royce which appeared in August 1919. A picture of tranquillity is painted as the chauffeur-driven Rolls glides through a forest.*

PRICE GUIDE **2**

ROLLS-ROYCE

"The Best Car in the World"

ROLLS-ROYCE, LIMITED

▲ *This advertisement for Vauxhall, entitled 'Sunshine after Storm', is, in the words of the advertiser, symbolic of the 1918 peace as well as the motor car.*

PRICE GUIDE **2**

◀ *An advertisement of 1919 extolling the virtues of the Humber – the car for the 'owner-driver'.*

PRICE GUIDE **2**

PRICE GUIDE

Automobile Accessories

Joseph Lucas of Birmingham was the most important British manufacturer of vehicle lamps. From 1901 he continued the development of lamps based on the principle of dropping water on to calcium carbide to produce acetylene gas. This burned with a brilliant white light which was a vast improvement on oil or candle headlamps. Lucas' 'King of the Road' headlamps appeared in 1905 costing £13 each and are popular collector's items today.

There were two types of acetylene headlamps: one was self-contained while the other had a generator, usually mounted on the running board, which produced the gas which was then fed to one or more projectors mounted on the front of the car. The second type was particularly favoured by French and American manufacturers.

Other manufacturers of highly collectable lamps include Powell & Hanmer, the Salisbury Company and Louis Blériot, the Frenchman, who was more famous as an aviator, but also made lights for cars like De Dion-Bouton, Léon-Bollée and Voisin.

The most famous of all car mascots was designed in 1910 by Charles Sykes. Called 'The Spirit of Ecstasy' it has adorned the front of every Rolls-Royce since. Among badges, the original RAC full members badge – a crowned motor wheel centred with a bust of Edward VII – is particulary prized.

▶ *Many car manufacturers produced stylish mascots to be fitted to the bonnets of their cars. This flying stork was the emblem for the Franco-Spanish company which made the Hispano-Suiza motor car.*

PRICE GUIDE ❻

▼ *Before he teamed up with Charles Rolls, Henry Royce had a factory in Manchester which produced electric motors. This cast aluminium plaque, c.1900, is from the top of a gear box.*

PRICE GUIDE ❺

◀ *This bakelite cigarette dispenser, c.1920, would have been attached to a car door or dashboard.*

PRICE GUIDE ❷

▶ *No early car would have been complete without a clock to tell the time. This brass clock fitted into the dashboard.*

PRICE GUIDE ❺

▶ *A chrome horse's head, c.1920, specially designed for a car owner to personalize his vehicle.*

PRICE GUIDE ❺

▶ *The Belgian company, Minerva, who built prestigious motor cars after World War I, chose the goddess Minerva as their mascot.*

PRICE GUIDE ❻

▲ *This nickel-plated female, poised as if ready to take flight, makes an elegant mascot.*

PRICE GUIDE ❺

PRICE GUIDE

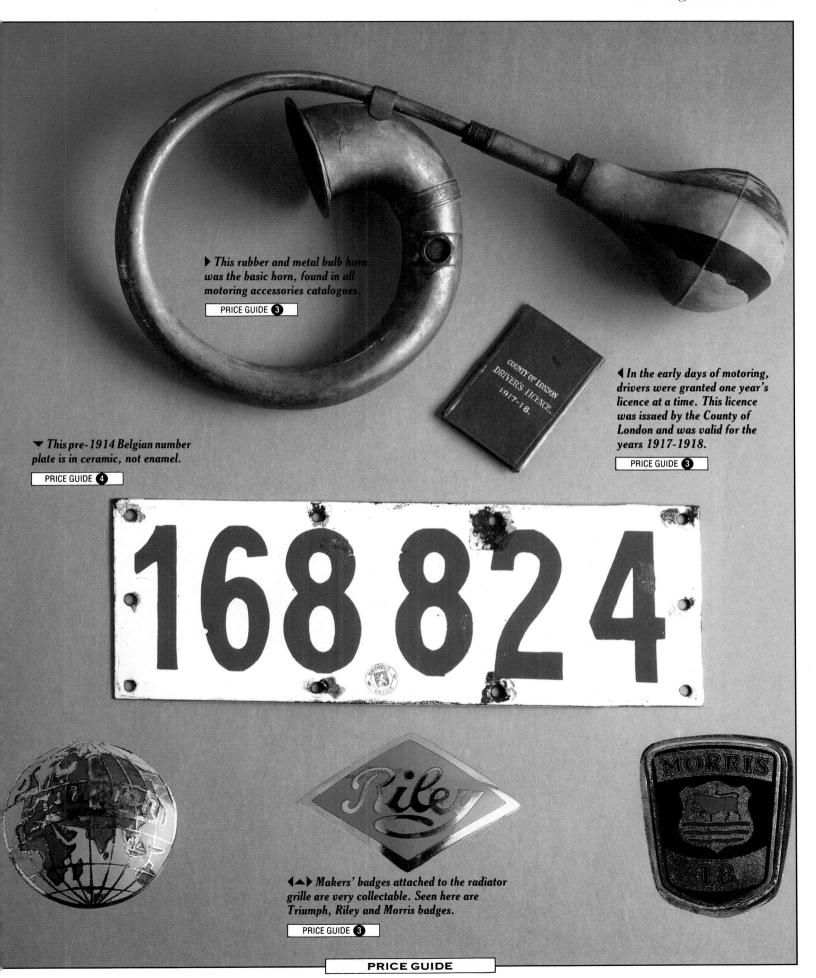

▶ *This rubber and metal bulb horn was the basic horn, found in all motoring accessories catalogues.*

PRICE GUIDE **3**

◀ *In the early days of motoring, drivers were granted one year's licence at a time. This licence was issued by the County of London and was valid for the years 1917-1918.*

PRICE GUIDE **3**

▼ *This pre-1914 Belgian number plate is in ceramic, not enamel.*

PRICE GUIDE **4**

◀▲▶ *Makers' badges attached to the radiator grille are very collectable. Seen here are Triumph, Riley and Morris badges.*

PRICE GUIDE **3**

PRICE GUIDE

COLLECTOR'S TIPS

COMPARISONS

Automobile Association

THE ENTWINED DOUBLE 'A' OF THE BRITISH AUTOMOBILE ASSOCIATION FIRST APPEARED IN ABOUT 1906. THE 1920S SIGN (LEFT) WAS FOUND ON AA TELEPHONE BOXES — THE GLASS BALLS REFLECTED THE LIGHT FROM HEADLAMPS AND SO COULD BE SPOTTED IN THE DARK. THE AA BADGE ON THE RIGHT, C.1914, WAS DISPLAYED ON THE CAR BONNET.

The beauty of motoring memorabilia is that it can cost the collector next to nothing or many thousands of pounds, depending on the areas explored. Postcard auctions produce a seemingly endless variety of photographs costing as little as 50 pence, although pictures with greater historical importance, for example recording a major motoring occasion, may cost up to £20. It is perhaps a sad reflection on human nature that photographs showing accidents are among the most popular with collectors.

BOOKS AND MAGAZINES

Books relating to motoring can still be found in jumble sales, car boot sales and second hand book shops, and picked up for a few pence. First editions of old books can, of course, be extremely expensive, and this is an area for the specialist. For the general collector, a good copy of *Through Persia in a Motor Car*, for instance, may be found for around £10, while *Pekin to Paris* by Luigi Barzini, complete with its map, might fetch twice as much.

'Association copies' of books are those with written comments or corrections in the margin, either by the author or the owner, or with inscriptions in the front by the author. These are particularly popular and very collectable.

Because of their flimsy construction, good early copies of motoring magazines are rare. A special collector's item is the edition of the first British weekly *The Autocar*, which was printed in red to celebrate the repeal of the Locomotives on Highways Act. A half year binding with covers and advertisements intact will fetch between £50 and £150 today depending on its condition.

ADVERTISEMENTS

Before the motoring press got into its stride, manufacturers like Benz, Daimler and De Dion advertised their cars with broadsheet advertisements posted unsolicited through likely letter boxes, exactly like today's junk mail. These advertisements are extremely rare and valuable now.

Car meets are good opportunities to buy accessories, and examine the details of unfamiliar artefacts. Lamps and other lighting equipment give a particularly wide field to the collector of accessories, and it is always interesting to see these fixed to the vehicle in the way that was intended.

Spirit of Ecstasy

IN THE EARLY DAYS OF MOTORING MANY CAR OWNERS PERSONALIZED THEIR VEHICLES WITH MASCOTS OF THEIR CHOICE. ALTHOUGH SOME WERE WELL DESIGNED AND WELL MADE, OTHERS WERE CHEAP AND GAUDY AND TOTALLY OUT OF KEEPING WITH THE CARS THEY ADORNED. IN 1910 THE DIRECTORS OF ROLLS-ROYCE, DISTRESSED AT SOME OF THE MASCOTS BEING DISPLAYED ON THEIR CARS, DECIDED TO DESIGN A DIGNIFIED MASCOT FOR THEIR CAR. THE ENGLISH SCULPTOR, CHARLES SYKES, WAS COMMISSIONED TO CREATE A SUITABLE EMBLEM AND THE 'SPIRIT OF ECSTASY' WAS BORN. THIS ELEGANT MASCOT HAS BEEN FITTED TO ROLLS-ROYCES EVER SINCE AND ALTHOUGH IT WAS NOT THE FIRST MANUFACTURERS' MASCOT, IT IS THE MOST FAMOUS.

① THE FAMOUS WINGED FIGURE WHICH HAS ADORNED THE ROLLS-ROYCE SINCE 1910.

② MOST PRE-1914 MODELS WERE SILVER PLATED: THIS BRONZE EXAMPLE IS UNUSUAL.

③ ROLLS-ROYCE PATENT MARK.

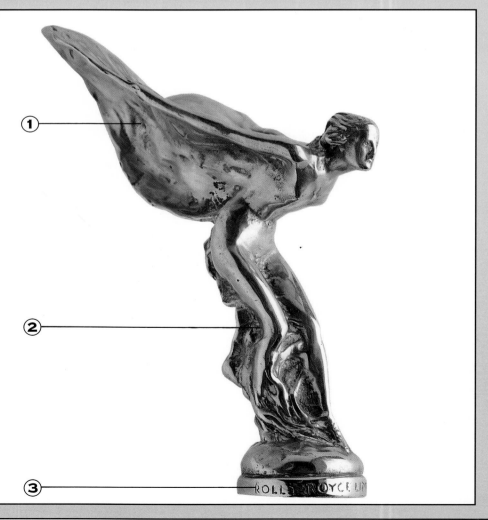

◆CLOSE UP◆

① PATENT MARK

② COUNTRY OF ISSUE

③ MANUFACTURER'S STAMP

④ MASCOT MODELLING

⑤ DRIVER'S LICENCE

⑥ MANUFACTURER'S PLATE

① THE PATENT MARKS OF THIS KEYLESS CLOCK APPEAR ON THE BOTTOM RIM.

④ THIS HORSE'S HEAD MASCOT HAS BEEN MODELLED WITH GREAT ATTENTION TO DETAIL.

② THE STAMP ON THIS NUMBER PLATE SHOWS THAT IT COMES FROM BELGIUM.

⑤ DRIVING LICENCE ISSUED TO A DR COLLIE BY THE COUNTY OF LONDON.

③ THE MANUFACTURER'S STAMP, EAGLER PAKMADE, SURROUNDS A SYMBOL OF AN EAGLE.

⑥ TECHNICAL DETAILS CAN BE FOUND ON THIS PLATE WHICH WAS ATTACHED TO A ROYCE GEAR BOX.

Before 1914 headlamps were not always sold as pairs, as there was no particular requirement for a car to have two headlamps. Today's collectors, however, greatly prefer pairs, and single examples may be had for a quarter of what a pair will fetch.

As well as headlamps these vintage cars would usually have side and rear lamps, which were often oil-powered even after 1900 when acetylene gas largely superceded oil for headlamps. The so-called 'opera lamps' had red, blue and sometimes green glass, and were used as courtesy lights for passengers getting out at the theatre or any other evening destination. The front and side glass of oil lamps is often hand cut and finished in nickel-plate or brass.

A pair of Lucas 'King of the Road' headlamps will fetch upwards of £1,000 today, while a single Powell & Hanmer can be had for around £400. A particularly fine pair of Badger Brass projectors made in America in 1905 sold recently for £1,200 without their gas generator. Oil lamps tend to be somewhat cheaper, and can be bought for between £80 and £300.

CAR ACCESSORIES

For those interested in accessories the mascots which were fixed to the radiator cap or further back on the bonnet provide another infinitely varied source. The very first manufacturer's mascot was made in 1903 by the Vulcan Motor Company, and represented, not surprisingly, Vulcan the Blacksmith. But before 1914 motorists usually preferred to choose their own personal mascot, and these appear in some quantity at auctions and with dealers specializing in automobilia.

POINTS TO WATCH

■ To protect original posters dealers usually back them with linen, or glaze and frame them. Modern reprints may be worth as little as a tenth of an original print.

■ The original AA badge, the so-called 'Stenson Cooke', has the signature of the first secretary of the Association embossed on the bracket, and is highly collectable. However, this badge has been reproduced recently, so look for a patina on the brass that only age can bring to check for authenticity.

■ Before 1914 Rolls-Royce mascots were often silver-plated; nickel-plating was used until the late 1920s. Replating, damage or bending will reduce the value of these mascots considerably.

■ Take care with all old photographs. They should be kept out of direct sunlight. If damaged, they can be backed with card and covered with a protective layer of plastic wrap. Specialists can produce copies and enlargements.

▼ *The early motorist invariably carried a spare can of petrol with him. Service stations and garages were few and far between. This Pratts can is dated around 1920.*

The Bicycle

The development of the safety bicycle at the end of the 19th century caused a social revolution, giving millions of city dwellers the freedom of the roads

The late Victorian and Edwardian eras were the golden age of the bicycle. In the 1870s and 1880s middle-class young men banded together in clubs, complete with a bugler to announce their coming, and explored leafy lanes – as yet untainted by the motor car – on high bicycles. By the 1890s, technical developments such as the introduction of the pneumatic tyre had made the safety bicycle the first affordable form of personal transport available to the working man, getting him to work and providing him with a cheap escape route into the countryside.

The bicycle is essentially a creation of the 19th century, although in 1966 a drawing of a rough prototype was found among the archives of Leonardo da Vinci (1452-1519). In the 18th century a few people experimented with man-powered carriages, known as manumotives (cranked by hand) or pedomotives (propelled by treadles). However, these were essentially rich men's playthings, requiring a servant or two to get them moving, and invariably had three or four wheels.

THE HOBBY HORSE

The first two-wheeled vehicle was patented by the German Baron von Drais in 1817. His 'running machine' consisted of two wooden wheels in line joined by a wooden board on which was mounted a saddle. The rider leaned forward, resting his arms on a padded leather 'balancing board', and moved by pushing off with each foot alternately in a motion very like that of an ice skater.

Other makers soon copied Drais's invention, which came to be known as a hobby-horse. Some improved on it; Dennis Johnson, of London, produced hobby-horses with a curved metal frame and larger wheels, for instance. Hobby-horse riding became a craze, especially among the young bucks of the Regency, but it did not last. The machines were certainly quick enough, regularly beating a coach-and-four in races, but they did not handle very well, and the appalling state of most of Europe's roads made them a very rough ride.

By 1821 the general enthusiasm for hobby-horses was at an end. Amateur and professional inventors turned their energies to perfecting the tricycle and the quadricycle. Some, such as Willard Sawyer, a

▶ *The invention of the safety bicycle and the pneumatic tyre made cycling an activity for both the sexes. In 1895, when this watercolour was painted, cycling had become a craze among the middle and upper classes, who promenaded gaily in the city streets.*

▼ *The Otto dicycle was a companionable two-wheeled alternative to the Ordinary in the 1880s.*

carpenter from Dover who produced many well-built wooden quadricycles in the 1850s and 1860s, achieved a measure of commercial success.

BONESHAKERS

In 1861, a pair of Parisian coach-builders called Ernest and Pierre Michaux produced a new form of machine which they called a velocipede. In appearance it was similar to the hobby-horse, but it was driven by pedal cranks which were attached to the hub of the front wheel.

Velocipedes became enormously popular in France, and the craze for them spread abroad in the late 1860s to England and the USA. They soon acquired the name 'boneshakers' in rueful tribute to the way the wooden wheels and the complete absence of suspension faithfully reproduced every jarring irregularity in the road surface.

Early machines, with their iron frames and metal-rimmed wheels of elm, ash and hickory, tended to be rigid and rather heavy; the average weight was around 60lbs (28kg). Their road-holding was not good, but improved dramatically with the introduction of solid rubber tyres in the late 1860s. The top speed that could be achieved in any comfort was around 8 m.p.h.

There were other disadvantages that prevented the boneshaker gaining wider acceptance. The front wheel pivoted as today for the purposes of steering, but since the pedals were mounted on it, it was almost impossible for a rider to turn a corner without fouling his legs on the rim. To prevent this, some manufacturers produced models with rear-wheel steering, but these proved unstable. An ingenious alternative was the Phantom, with a fixed front wheel but a frame hinged straight down the middle. Although the Phantom cornered well, it took a good rider to prevent it jack-knifing while travelling in a straight line.

Mounting a boneshaker required some athleticism; the approved method was to run alongside the machine and then vault into the saddle. Later, a step was provided so

machine. Many such large-wheel models were displayed at a show in Paris in 1869. However, the Franco-Prussian War of 1870 effectively destroyed the French velocipede industry before these new models could make an impact, and elsewhere the craze ran its course, dying down by 1871.

THE ORDINARY

With the eclipse of France, further development of the bicycle switched to England where, in the 1870s, the high bicycle was developed. In the interests of increased speed and efficiency the front wheel got larger and larger – ultimately the only limit was the length of the rider's legs, and wheels of up to 60 inches (1.5 metres) in diameter were made. At the same time the rear wheel, its function reduced to that of a balance, was made smaller and smaller, creating the shape known at the time as an Ordinary but later as the penny-farthing.

The wheels had tensioned steel spokes and rubber-covered metal rims while the frames were made of tubular steel for lightness and manoeuvrability; the average Ordinary weighed around 40lbs (18kg), racing models half that. Ordinary racing was an exciting spectator sport, with the best machines able to sustain speeds of

20 m.p.h. over quite considerable distances.

To get the right leverage on the pedals, the saddles of Ordinaries were mounted almost directly above the hub of the big wheel. Some people, however, were willing to sacrifice a little speed in exchange for a less perilous perch than this.

Two successful models, the Singer Xtraordinary and the Beale and Straw Facile, catered for these timorous souls by replacing the rotating pedals with a treadle and lever system. This allowed the cycle to be propelled by a swinging, to and fro motion of the feet and for the saddle to be set further back. The system was very efficient and several endurance records were set on an Xtraordinary.

In 1884, the firm of Hillman, Herbert and Beale introduced the Kangaroo, which had a geared chain drive fitted to the front wheel. Chain drives had long been used on tricycles but this was the first time one had been used on a bicycle. The innovation was immediately copied by other manufacturers, but the same year also saw the first popular rear-wheel drive safety bicycle, which in the space of just ten years or so consigned the Ordinary and its kin to history although they continued to be made for a small band of enthusiasts into the 20th century.

that riders could mount by scooting along with one foot then swinging themselves into the saddle.

The lack of any gearing on the front wheel meant that the rider had to pedal furiously to increase speed or to get up even a slight incline, while going downhill he had to lift his legs on to a foot-rest in front of the handlebars lest his legs get tangled in the flying pedals.

One way of increasing speed was to increase the size of the drive wheel. The provision of a mounting step had made this possible, while in 1869 another Parisian, Meyer, patented the wire-spoked wheel, permitting wheels to grow large while not appreciably increasing the weight of the

▶ *This hobby-horse is English, and was made in 1820 by a smith or a wheelwright. Unusually, it is steered with handlebars rather than a tiller.*

▶ *The front wheel of this racing Ordinary is 5ft 3ins (1.6m) in diameter. It was made in 1885 by the Coventry Machinists Company.*

▼ *This velocipede was made by Michaux in 1868. It has bob pedals, weighted on one side to keep the flat surface uppermost.*

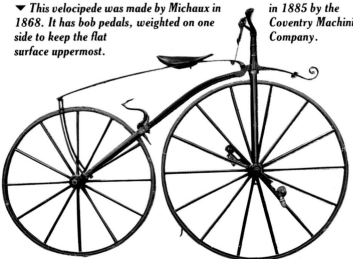

Lady's Rover

THIS ROVER, MADE IN 1891, IS ONE OF THE EARLIEST EXAMPLES OF A DROP-FRAME SAFETY BICYCLE, ONE IN WHICH THE CROSS-BAR HAS BEEN REMOVED IN ORDER TO ACCOMMODATE A LADY'S SKIRTS. AS A FURTHER SAFEGUARD, STRANDS OF THREAD HAVE BEEN STRETCHED FROM THE REAR WHEEL HUB OVER THE MUDGUARD TO PREVENT A DRESS FROM BEING FOULED BY THE SPOKES.

THE WHEELS HAVE TANGENTIAL SPOKES AND SOLID TYRES. THE ARAB-SPRUNG SADDLE IS DESIGNED TO ABSORB SOME OF THE SHOCK

TRANSMITTED BY THE RUBBER TYRES. THERE IS A SPOON BRAKE ON THE FRONT WHEEL, OPERATED BY A LARGE LEVER SITUATED BELOW THE HANDLEBARS. THE FRAME IS OF TUBULAR STEEL, WITH A RAKISH CURVE TO THE FRONT FORKS AND A BOTTOM TUBE WHICH FOLLOWS THE CONTOURS OF THE FRONT WHEEL. AS A FURTHER SAFETY FEATURE, THE CHAIN IS GUARDED BY A METAL FRAME COVERED WITH A PIECE OF LEATHER. THE MAKER'S NAME IS ON A METAL ESCUTCHEON ON THE STEERING COLUMN.

① SPRUNG SADDLE

② PLUNGER BRAKE

③ CURVED FRONT FORKS

④ DRESS CORD, TO PROTECT WOMEN'S CLOTHING FROM SPOKES

⑤ CHAIN GUARD

Twin-Wheel Cycle

A SHORT-LIVED ATTEMPT TO COMBINE THE STABILITY OF A TRICYCLE WITH THE WIDTH OF A BICYCLE, TWIN-WHEELS WERE ONLY MADE FOR WOMEN, AND ALWAYS HAD DROP FRAMES AND DRESS CORDS. THE REAR WHEELS HAVE ONE HUB, WITH A CENTRAL SPROCKET WHEEL. THIS EXAMPLE DATES FROM 1900.

The safety bicycle was so-called to contrast it with the Ordinary, whose riders were always in danger of 'coming a cropper' – pitching headlong over the handlebars – whenever the big wheel hit an obstacle, such as a large stone or a deep pothole. Sometimes a rider could be flung to the ground simply because of his over-enthusiastic use of the spoon brake typical of such machines.

What made safeties safe was the introduction of the rear-wheel chain drive. This not only meant that the wheels could be geared, obviating the necessity for large diameters, but also that the pedals, and thus the saddle,

could be mounted between the wheels, giving the bicycles much greater stability.

The first model to be made on this principle was the Tangent and Coventry Tricycle Company's Bicyclette in 1879. Perhaps ahead of its time, the Bicyclette did not achieve any great sales – though it did add a new word to the French language – and it was not until 1885 that the chain-driven safety bicycle made its breakthrough.

Several manufacturers produced models at this time but the one that captured the popular imagination was Sutton and Starley's Rover, which set new speed records that year.

·PRICE GUIDE·

Early Bicycles

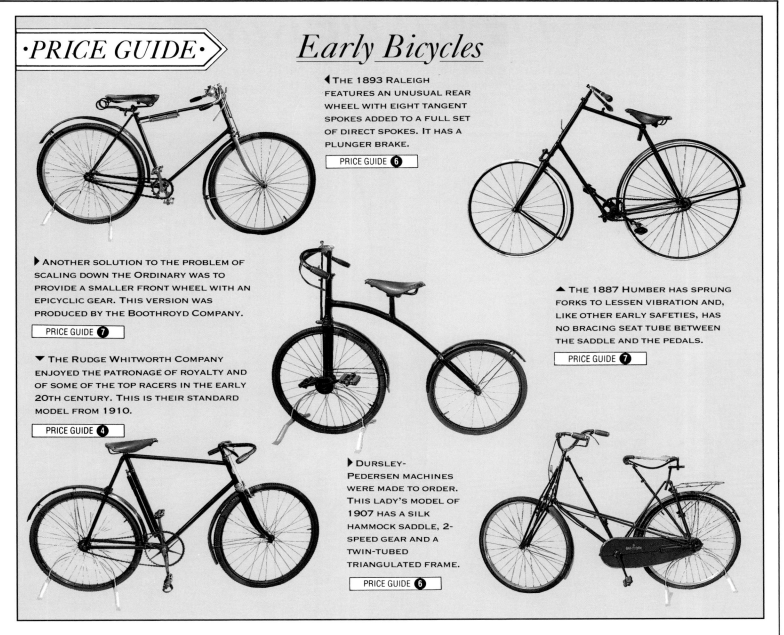

◀ THE 1893 RALEIGH FEATURES AN UNUSUAL REAR WHEEL WITH EIGHT TANGENT SPOKES ADDED TO A FULL SET OF DIRECT SPOKES. IT HAS A PLUNGER BRAKE.

PRICE GUIDE **6**

▶ ANOTHER SOLUTION TO THE PROBLEM OF SCALING DOWN THE ORDINARY WAS TO PROVIDE A SMALLER FRONT WHEEL WITH AN EPICYCLIC GEAR. THIS VERSION WAS PRODUCED BY THE BOOTHROYD COMPANY.

PRICE GUIDE **7**

▼ THE RUDGE WHITWORTH COMPANY ENJOYED THE PATRONAGE OF ROYALTY AND OF SOME OF THE TOP RACERS IN THE EARLY 20TH CENTURY. THIS IS THEIR STANDARD MODEL FROM 1910.

PRICE GUIDE **4**

▲ THE 1887 HUMBER HAS SPRUNG FORKS TO LESSEN VIBRATION AND, LIKE OTHER EARLY SAFETIES, HAS NO BRACING SEAT TUBE BETWEEN THE SADDLE AND THE PEDALS.

PRICE GUIDE **7**

▶ DURSLEY-PEDERSEN MACHINES WERE MADE TO ORDER. THIS LADY'S MODEL OF 1907 HAS A SILK HAMMOCK SADDLE, 2-SPEED GEAR AND A TWIN-TUBED TRIANGULATED FRAME.

PRICE GUIDE **6**

The Rover had wheels of almost equal size and a frame of tubular steel. The crossbar, rear forks, and the two stays joining the chain wheel to the rear hub and the front forks formed a diamond shape, which gave the bicycle a great deal of stability and rigidity without seriously increasing its weight. This pattern soon became standard.

Being closer to the ground was not without its disadvantages. Early safety bicycles shook the bones almost as much as had velocipedes. Some of this discomfort was allayed by sprung saddles, but there was nothing to prevent the continuous jarring of the arms and shoulders from the handlebars.

Some models of the early 1880s included various mechanical contrivances to deal with this problem, including ingenious fully-sprung frames, but it was not completely solved until Dunlop's invention of the pneumatic tyre, first used in 1889 and universal on bicycles by 1895.

Crossbars were omitted from the frames of some of the first safeties to make drop-frame models, the first bicycles ever made with women in mind. In England prior to the 1890s – and for long after in some quarters – it was considered indecorous and even gynaecologically reckless for women to ride. Even at the height of the

velocipede craze in France, women rarely rode outside the raffish milieux of the race-track, music hall or circus.

In England, custom and codes of dress as much as danger and physical incapacity prevented women from riding, and when they began to do so in the 1890s some took to wearing knicker-bockers and bloomers, scandalizing many of the older generation but helping to liberate women from the worst excesses of Victorian corsetry.

Many of the objections to women riders were forgotten after 1895, when a craze for bicycling among upper-class ladies gave women's riding a new respectability.

POINTS TO WATCH

■ The best way to develop an interest in early bicycles and to gain experience of old machines is to join one of the many Veteran Cycle Clubs.

■ Machines made before World War I in good condition are expensive and hard to find. Collecting them is usually a matter of finding and restoring discarded machines, but much of this can be quite easily done at home with rust remover and simple tools.

■ Look for the manufacturer's name stamped on the back of the seat spring.

■ Pluck metal wheel spokes; they should all be tight and give off the same note.

A Day at the Races

The excitement of going to the races was only partly to do with the
horses – it was also the social event of the season

Going to the races was a popular diversion for all classes of society. King Edward's personal interest in the Turf gave the sport a respectability it had lacked throughout the 19th century, and by 1900 most courses had been enclosed which kept the rough elements at bay. Entry prices were staggered to appeal to the different sectors of society, and ranged from a £4 voucher for the Royal Enclosure at Ascot, to the standard one shilling gate fee that every worker could afford. The lower classes were entertained at the gaming tables and beer booths, while the aristocracy paraded on lawns in front of the grandstand. Only in the paddock and at the bookmakers did the classes mingle. Large sums of money were staked and lost on horses; King Edward placed huge bets on his own runners, and even opponents were delighted when a royal favourite came home.

Punters of all classes line up to place bets on the tote. Segregated elsewhere on the racecourse, here landlords rubbed shoulders with their tenants.

▲ *The illustrated press of the early 1900s were as hungry for pictures of royalty as their modern counterparts. This issue of* The Daily Graphic *celebrates the first ever Derby win by a ruling monarch, Edward VII in 1909, when his horse* Minoru *romped home.*

Horse racing was Edward VII's favourite spectator sport. Nothing gave him greater pleasure than perusing bloodstock in the paddock and placing bets on likely royal winners. Even on his deathbed in 1910, his last words were of delight at the news that 'Witch of the Air', a favourite filly, had triumphed that afternoon at Kempton Park.

For King Edward, a day at the races was an excuse to abandon affairs of state and indulge in the pleasures of sport and speculation. He went to every meeting where he had a runner that was in with a chance, and he placed very handsome bets on his own horses. Queen Victoria had scowled at these disreputable activities, but from 1901-1910, King Edward's patronage of the Turf gave racing a respectability it had previously lacked.

SOCIETY EVENTS

The top Edwardian race meetings were grand society events, and it was a social duty to be seen at Epsom on Derby Day, at Goodwood, and above all at Ascot. The aristocracy went because they followed the King. Local landowners went because they wished to assert their position in the social hierarchy. Members of Parliament went to parade in front of their constituents. And those who had social aspirations went because everyone of any consequence was also there.

These elegant society spectacles were very different from the rowdy and debauched race meetings of the mid-19th century. The Victorian middle classes considered racing morally reprehensible, patronized

▲ *An enthusiast studies the racing pages, oblivious to the boredom of his companion who would prefer to join the crowd of fashionable racegoers strolling round the paddock.*

▶ *A day at the races was a major social event, and for the well-heeled it was a chance to parade in all their finery. Fashions were bought from top Parisian couturiers and Edwardian ladies were at pains to match hats, fans and jewellery to the day's outfits, knowing that as many eyes would be on them as on the horses.*

only by the idle rich and the lower classes. Open meetings were undoubtedly a magnet for crooks, thugs, pickpockets and prostitutes and lurid tales of rioting, corruption, and worse still, public copulation, were enough to keep the prurient middle class at home. By 1900, however, the sport had been tamed. Most courses had been enclosed and every spectator paid an entrance fee on the gate, so that revenue from beer and gambling booths was less important to the organizers.

Known thieves and thugs could be barred from enclosed courses. But more importantly, the 'riff raff' were kept out of the exclusive stands by a differential pricing policy. The grandstand cost twice as much as the paddock, and the paddock twice as much as the second class enclosure.

CLASS SEGREGATION

This segregation meant that all classes could attend race meetings with propriety. As a landlord, there was no danger of finding yourself seated next to one of your tenants or estate workers. In between races, of course, gentlemen strolled down to the paddock and chatted with jockeys, trainers, tipsters and bookmakers. But the conversation adhered rigidly to Turf matters; a duke never invited his jockey to dine in the evening.

The racing day began early for the traders and barrow boys arriving with cartloads of spices, candies, cider, lemonade and beer, and for the itinerant gamesters, entertainers and musicians. At about noon, the crowds began to disgorge from the local railway station. Hansom cabs transporting rail travellers to the course jostled with donkey carts, tandems and phaetons on the road. The 'yellow Earl', Lord Lonsdale, an expert sportsman and president of the National Sporting Club, could be spotted in the maelstrom, smoking a long cigar in his bright yellow phaeton.

Other wealthy aristocrats arrived by motor car and from 1905 Ascot had a special enclosure behind the grandstand for King Edward's 40hp Mercedes and other automobiles. It was a journey fraught with obstacles – not least the policemen waiting to fine drivers who exceeded the 12 m.p.h. speed limit, and the clouds of dust which ruined the sometimes elaborate racing outfits. Female 'motoristes' had to wear full-length dustcoats, and some sported goggles and cloth caps like the men. 'A little drawer beneath the seat is the secret of the dainty motoriste' advised Dorothy Levitt. 'In its recesses put clean gloves, veil, handkerchief, powder-puff, pins, hairpins and a hand-mirror. Some chocolates are very soothing sometimes'. Miss Levitt also advised an automatic colt revolver in the cosmetic box, as a defence against possible surprise attacks

▲ *Each racehorse owner decided on his own racing colours to be worn by the jockey. Bright colours, such as the scarlet silk of this cap, and bold designs were usually chosen so that spectators could easily distinguish the runner of their fancy.*

LIFE AND LEISURE

Derby Day

▲ PERSIMMON WINS THE 1896 DERBY, TO THE HUGE EXCITEMENT OF THE CROWDS WATCHING THE SUPREME TEST FOR THREE-YEAR-OLDS.

▶ THE DERBY BECAME AN UNOFFICIAL FÊTE FOR LONDON WORKERS, WHO CONSIDERED THE LOSS OF A DAY'S PAY WELL WORTH THE JAMBOREE.

ROYAL ASCOT WAS THE MOST EXCLUSIVE EDWARDIAN RACE MEETING, BUT THE DERBY WAS UNDOUBTEDLY THE MOST COVETED PRIZE OF THE BRITISH TURF. THE DERBY WINNER WAS ALWAYS CONSIDERED THE CHAMPION THREE-YEAR-OLD, SO THE BEST HORSES AND THE BIGGEST CROWD WERE ATTRACTED TO EPSOM. INAUGURATED BY LORD DERBY AND FIRST RUN ON MAY 4 IN 1780, THE RACE ATTRACTED UP TO 70,000 SPECTATORS OF ALL CLASSES, WHO FLOCKED TO THE DOWNS BY RAIL OR ROAD FOR THE FASTEST FLAT RACE IN BRITAIN.

HALF THE FUN OF THE OUTING WAS WATCHING COSTERS' CARTS AND PONY TRAPS MINGLE WITH THE FOUR-HORSE CARRIAGES OF THE ARISTOCRACY. THE DOWNLAND SETTING WAS A HAZARD FOR THESE VEHICLES AND THERE WERE COUNTLESS ACCIDENTS AS THEY CAREERED DOWNHILL AT FULL GALLOP IN ORDER TO GET UP THE OTHER SIDE. KING EDWARD'S TRIUMPHS AT EPSOM IN 1900 AND 1909 WERE GREETED WITH A STANDING OVATION.

often in lonely and little trafficked country lanes.

Ladies who owned their own racehorses were considered rather 'fast' in the late Victorian era, and often had to assume male pseudonyms; Lily Langtry, for example, raced as 'Mr Jersey'. But by 1900 society's attitudes had relaxed, and some 81 ladies had registered racing colours. To the vast majority of female racegoers, however, 'good form' meant knowing what to wear. Having a little flutter and marking the racecard was amusing, but the real business of the day was to discover what the Parisian couturiers had decreed to be fashionable.

ASCOT

The very best dresses, of course, were reserved for Ascot. Each meeting had its own style and ambience. Some preferred the 'patrician and plebeian' spectacle of Derby Day, and some the relaxed and friendly atmosphere of Newmarket. But Royal Ascot was unanimously considered the peak of the social season.

It was also the great watershed. A voucher for the Royal Enclosure was really a certificate of social acceptability, and Lord Randolph Churchill had the task of casting out undesirables. He sorted the applications into three categories – 'certainly', 'perhaps', and 'certainly not' – and it was a job which, as he joked himself, made him the best-hated and best-loved man in the country.

In 1903, expecting King Edward's popularity to boost attendances, Lord Randolph raised the price of the Ascot Royal Enclosure voucher from £1 to £4 – to little avail. The *haut monde* thronged to see the King and Queen, and new stands were erected to celebrate Edward's first Ascot as King.

During Ascot week, the royal couple entertained a large house party at Windsor Castle. Carriages and motor cars left Windsor for the course at 12.15 each day. The first race was at 1.30, after which there was an hour for lunch – prawns and plover's eggs for the King, dispatched daily from Windsor. New reception rooms and a grand luncheon room in white with green satin panels had been built to cope with the volume of royal entertaining, and the view out of the rostrum was enlivened by a parterre of

▲ *The runners are led down to the start, their jockeys dressed in vivid racing silks and their trainers ready to give last-minute advice on the conditions of the turf.*

▼ *Excitement grows as horses thunder down the race-track, and the crowds press forward to see them clear the fences.*

colourful rhododendrons, artistically arranged.

From the grandstand, the lawns were a dazzling spectacle, and burst into bloom as the ladies opened their silk parasols. Hyacinth, lettuce-green, champagne, peach and pigeon's egg were the fashionable pastel shades, enlivened by the dramatic parma and black and white magpie combination favoured by Queen Alexandra. The Queen was a fashion barometer and popularized the boa of silk flower petals or marabou and ostrich feathers which racegoers wore dangling to mid-thigh.

Ascot gowns were extravagant creations of foulard and silk taffetas with layers of diaphanous overdresses, trimmed with valuable antique lace, velvet ribbons and appliqués of crystal and steel-bead embroidery. They were worn with gloves and a huge picture hat, overflowing with silk flowers and drooping ostrich plumes. The gowns – 'tatters' in Edwardian slang – were commissioned at huge expense from top Parisian couturiers like Maison Worth, Mme Paquin, Mme Chéruit and the Soeurs Callot. One English couturier, Lady Lucy Duff Gordon or 'Lucile', rose to international fame during the era, and dressed certain members of the English aristocracy including Princess Alice, the Duchess of Westminster and Margot Asquith. Lucile immortalized her dresses with romantic titles like 'The Sighing Sounds of Lips Unsatisfied'.

These 'tatters' were the talking point of the lady spectators, and of society journalists who rushed detailed descriptions of the Ascot fashions to the illustrated press. Society gossip and fashion were generally better understood than matters of the Turf – even amongst some of the men. The pages of

▲ *What is now the Royal Enclosure used to have a separate stand for the staff, known as the Royal Household Enclosure. Tickets for the paddock were issued separately.*

▼ *Edward VII at his last Derby, waiting to lead in Minoru after his victory.*

Those not invited to Windsor for Ascot week took houses on the river, in the 18th-century tradition. On Ascot Sunday, all the house parties congregated at Boulter's Lock on the Thames and, weather permitting, spent the day boating.

THE END OF AN ERA

The gilded existence continued until 1910, when Ascot happened to fall a few weeks after King Edward's death. The racecards that year were black-edged, the blinds of the royal box were drawn, and everyone in the Royal enclosure wore full mourning. After that, racing was never quite the same. In 1915, the sport was a prime target in the battle of values, and race meetings were finally suspended throughout the war years.

Punch, for instance, satirized the social-climbing Bullyon Boundermere family who lost a sizeable fortune at Ascot by only betting on horses which were owned by dukes.

The races were really an excuse for lavish entertaining. At Goodwood, society gathered at the Duke of Richmond's home and other local house parties, and occasionally sought 'regilding' among the company of American millionaires staying at the Hotel Metropole in Brighton. The Metropole's Restaurant des Ambassadeurs was the most exclusive venue for dinner after a day at Goodwood.

LIFE AND LEISURE

Shooting Weekends

RACE MEETINGS OCCUPIED THE SPRING AND SUMMER MONTHS OF THE SOCIAL CALENDAR. DURING THE AUTUMN AND WINTER, EDWARDIAN SOCIETY GATHERED IN LARGE HOUSE PARTIES TO SPEND THE WEEKEND HUNTING AND SHOOTING. THESE SPORTS WERE RULED BY SOCIAL SNOBBERY, AND TO HUNT WITH A 'PROVINCIAL' PACK OR ROUGH SHOOT OVER DOGS WAS TO INVITE SCORN. DRIVEN SHOOTS WERE CONSIDERED FASHIONABLE AND THE KILLING OF AS MANY BIRDS AS POSSIBLE WAS GOOD SPORT.

IF A GAMEKEEPER THOUGHT THE PHEASANTS WERE LOOKING SOMEWHAT THIN ON THE GROUND, THOUSANDS COULD BE SMUGGLED IN BY RAIL BEFORE THE GUESTS ARRIVED. KING EDWARD WAS A KEEN SHOT HIMSELF AND ORGANIZED LARGE SHOOTING PARTIES AT BALMORAL AND SANDRINGHAM. LADIES JOINED IN THE ACTIVITIES, ALTHOUGH MOST WERE CONTENT TO PROVIDE A DECORATIVE ELEMENT TO THE WEEKENDS AND BROUGHT UP TO 15 DIFFERENT OUTFITS TO COPE WITH THE FOUR OR FIVE COSTUME CHANGES A DAY.

▲ THE QUINTESSENTIAL ENGLISH COUNTRY PURSUITS OF HUNTING AND SHOOTING REACHED A PEAK OF POPULARITY DURING EDWARD VII'S REIGN, AND COUNTRY HOUSE WEEKENDS BECAME VERY FASHIONABLE AMONG HIGH SOCIETY.

Binoculars

The first successful versions of modern binoculars were made in the early 1800s, and by the Edwardian period there were many styles to choose from

The 'sporting monarch', King Edward VII, was an ardent racing fan who also owned a string of racehorses, and it was his royal patronage which made racing such a popular event in the Edwardian period. Race meetings were always colourful spectacles, with the ladies and gentlemen dressed in the latest extravagant fashions. However, no matter what they wore, no serious racegoer's outfit was complete without a pair of binoculars to view the race in progress.

Modern binoculars are so commonplace that we take them for granted, but the precision instruments in use today are the result of centuries of slow and painstaking experiments made by scientists at work all over Europe.

The first telescope, from which 'binocles' or binocular glasses evolved, is said to have been made by 'an obscure spectacle maker' from the Dutch town of Middleburg in 1608. Described more patronizingly as 'an illiterate mechanik', Hans Lippershey showed his invention to the celebrated general, Prince Maurice of Nassau, who was so impressed that the inventor was asked to produce a double version of the same instrument. But this was easier said than done and, apart from some attempts by a group of Capuchin monks before 1700, no practical efforts to produce a binocular telescope were made again until the early 19th century.

'LONG JOHN' GLASSES

A Viennese optician called Johann Friedrich Voigt-länder is credited with producing the first low magnification opera glasses in 1823. Two years later, J. P. Lemière patented his own version of modern field glasses using a pair of Galilean telescopes that could be focussed together. They were imported into England from France in large numbers and were still in use in the Edwardian age. Known also as 'Long John' glasses, their barrels could be well over a foot (30cm) in length, though the longest binoculars ever produced were probably the six-foot (183cm) variety made by the Japanese for German U-boats in World War I. Sometimes foldable, pocket versions of Galilean binoculars were made but glasses with this unwieldy optical system are now rarely seen outside museums and specialist antique shops.

ACHROMATIC LENS

Throughout the second half of the 19th century, professional and amateur opticians continued to bring out field glass lenses which gave greater and more accurate magnification. One of the most important innovations was the achromatic lens. Used in all the most fashionable sporting and military field glasses

▼ *No day at the races was complete without a pair of binoculars through which to view the horses. A keen racegoer, Edward VII is seen here, with binoculars in hand, at the Derby in April 1902.*

▲ *The telescope was the forerunner of binocular glasses. This 17th century telescope belonged to Sir Isaac Newton.*

A PAIR OF BRASS AND LEATHER BINOCULARS, C.1910. THESE WERE MADE SPECIFICALLY FOR USE BY RACE OFFICIALS AND STEWARDS.

ALSO DESIGNED FOR STEWARDS, THESE BRASS AND LEATHER BINOCULARS WERE MADE IN THE EARLY 1900s.

THIS PAIR OF ELEGANT EDWARDIAN BINOCULARS USED BY RACE TRACK OFFICIALS ARE MADE ENTIRELY OF BRASS.

from the mid-19th century to the 1890s, these lenses helped to cut out the colour distortions which had dogged the older makes for so long.

In the 1860s, J. H. Steward's catalogues advertised 'binocular field, race, marine, tourist or landscape glasses' with six or sometimes 12 achromatic lenses. With shorter bodies than the Galilean type, they came in many different magnification strengths, sizes and weights. Most of the Steward's field glasses had barrels of black japanned brass covered in Morocco leather and were sold with optional sun or spray shades.

The most expensive binoculars in Steward's 1867 catalogue were a pair of men's 'field/race glasses' made of aluminium which cost 12 guineas. One of the firm's 'newly improved' binoculars had changeable eye-pieces of three different powers: one for the theatre, one for 'field' use (including horse-racing), and the last for use at sea. With these, one was supposed to be able to see people walking at a distance of six miles (10km), houses 10 miles (16km) away and churches at 18 miles (29km).

'PORRO' PRISM BINOCULARS

However, the real breakthrough in the optics and design of field glasses came when Carl Zeiss first marketed prism binoculars in the 1890s. Invented by an Italian scientist, Ignazio Porro, in 1851 but neglected due to lack of suitable glass, the 'Porro' prism system meant that binoculars could be more powerful as well as more compact than ever before. A triangular prism in each barrel reflected the light beam twice and turned the image the right way up without the aid of a negative, concave lens. Much more complex than the traditional low-magnification field glasses, they often had four lenses in the eye-pieces alone. The 'objective' lenses which received the light at the end furthest from the face had two sections and could be placed wider apart than the eye-pieces, giving prismatic binoculars their characteristic shoulder-shaped barrels. The use of prisms also increased the overall stereoscopic effect and widened the field of view.

Another new type of binocular using a 'roof' prism was developed at much the same time. This system was invented by a German optician called Carl Hensoldt in 1897. Roof prisms were manufactured commercially by M. Hensoldt und Söhne in their popular 'Dialyt' field glasses from 1905. The introduction of the roof prism was a further refinement on Porro's invention and allowed field glasses to be made with even slimmer barrels. Miniature and compact binoculars in which the barrels folded

·PRICE GUIDE· FIELD GLASSES

Field glasses are obviously worth more if they are in good condition and still have their original cases. The best places to find them are at dealers specializing in optical or scientific instruments.

◀ *Even a blustery, rainy day would not put off the real racing enthusiasts. Dressed in the height of fashion, the spectators in the grandstand could watch the races through binoculars.*

▶ *Going to the races was no casual affair. Not only did women dress smartly, but gentlemen racegoers also dressed elegantly, particularly in the members' enclosure, where top hats, white gloves and binoculars were de rigueur.*

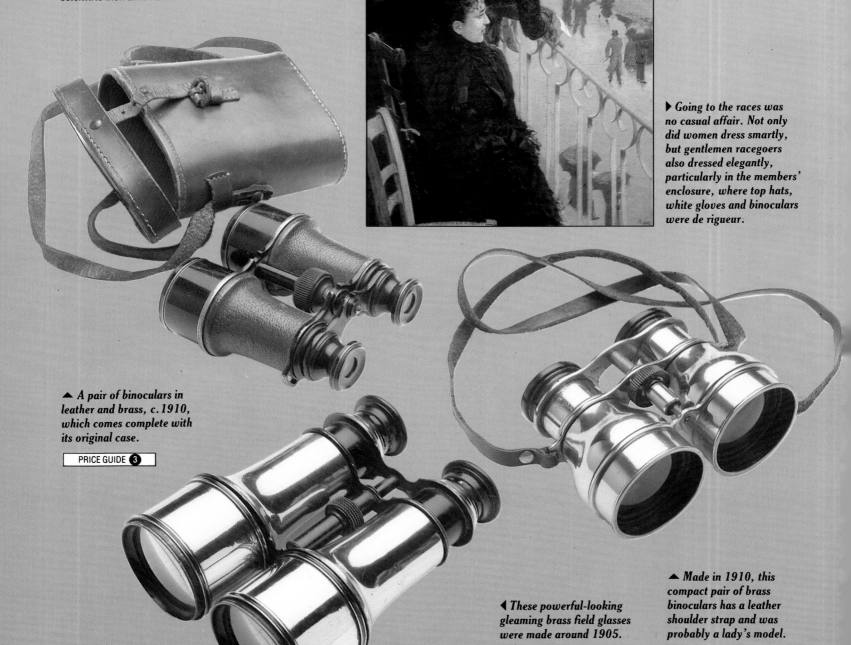

▲ *A pair of binoculars in leather and brass, c.1910, which comes complete with its original case.*

PRICE GUIDE ❸

◀ *These powerful-looking gleaming brass field glasses were made around 1905.*

PRICE GUIDE ❸

▲ *Made in 1910, this compact pair of brass binoculars has a leather shoulder strap and was probably a lady's model.*

PRICE GUIDE ❸

inwards for easy storage became very popular from that time onwards.

The Edwardians bought their field glasses from a variety of outlets. These could have included one of the well-known optical instrument makers based in London such as James Aitchison (now Dolland and Aitchison), Ross Ltd, J. H. Steward, Negretti and Zambra, or Carl Zeiss. Based at Jena in Saxe-Weimar (which later became part of the German Democratic Republic), Zeiss had a branch in London from the 1890s. Steward had branches in the Scilly Islands, Australia, South Africa and India. But in Britain binoculars were also sold by ordinary opticians' and chemists' shops.

A large number of binoculars stamped with English dealers' names were in fact made abroad. The most popular foreign makes came from Germany where the techniques of grinding glass were much more advanced than anywhere else. But though German factories once made a practice of engraving their field glasses with serial numbers, it is usually very difficult to trace the location and date of their manufacture.

Many of the field glasses used by early 20th-century racegoers were originally developed for military operations in the Boer and Afghan wars. In fact, the popularity of Zeiss binoculars in Edwardian England was largely due to the fact that Boer farmers had used them to outwit less well-equipped British troops in South Africa. Trieder field glasses made in Berlin and supplied to the German army were promoted for sporting use to English customers in *The Art Annual* in 1900.

Field glasses for women were sometimes quite ornate, with gilt decorations embossed into their leather barrels. Usually lighter in weight than those made for men, they were often intended for use at the theatre and opera as well as at sporting events. Indeed, Edwardian women frequently used their jewelled opera glasses while spectating at horse races.

BARREL COVERINGS

Fashions in binoculars' barrel coverings did not change very much between the 1860s and 1910, and they were usually of black leather or metal. Like the army binoculars which gave them their name, field glasses for men and women were sold with hard leather sling cases lined with a softer leather, leatherette or textile. Sometimes, men's binocular cases imitated the oval shape of leather hairbrush cases.

Though the term 'field glasses' is often used nowadays to distinguish low-powered glasses from prismatic binoculars, this has never been a hard-and-fast rule. In any case, by the early 1900s both types involved a high degree of precision engineering. Occasionally dealers would illustrate their products' complicated internal workings in magazine advertisements. Apart from several different kinds of ground glass for the lenses, these consisted typically of a sheet of rolled brass, cast aluminium for the barrel casings, mild steel and brass rods, galvanized steel washers and ribbon steel springs.

▲ An elegant pair of brass binoculars made in Paris c.1910.

PRICE GUIDE 4

▲ These brass and leather binoculars were made in 1908 and fit neatly into their original leather carrying case.

PRICE GUIDE 3

Sporting Cigarette Cards

Sports, such as football, cricket and racing, are among the most popular
of the many cigarette card subjects which reflect the predominance of
male smokers in the Edwardian era

The origins of the cigarette card can
be traced to France where in the
1840s some shops started giving
away business cards to remind customers
where to find particular goods or services.
In an effort to ensure that the cards were not
immediately thrown away, many retailers
decorated their cards with fine engravings of
subjects connected with their business.

COLLECTABLE SETS

A further incentive for customers to return
was provided when firms started producing
collectable sets of cards, often superbly
printed in colour. Then, instead of using
illustrations associated with their business,
shops started producing cards decorated
with any subject that they thought would
appeal to people. Since their customers
were mainly women, children, fashion and
flowers were among the most popular
subjects. This practice spread to other
European countries and, in the 1870s,
across the Atlantic to the United States.

Although trade cards were, at first,
issued by shops, product manufacturers
soon saw the advantages of issuing cards
too. If buyers found the cards attractive,
they would purchase more of the firms'
goods in order to add to their collections.

Like the cards used to promote other
products, the first cigarette cards were
separate items, given away by the shop
when a purchase was made. They first
found their way into cigarette packs in the
United States, where the sale of tobacco
products was increasing rapidly in the
1870s. Cigarettes were sold in paper packs,
with a cardboard stiffener to prevent
crushing. Then, around 1878, someone

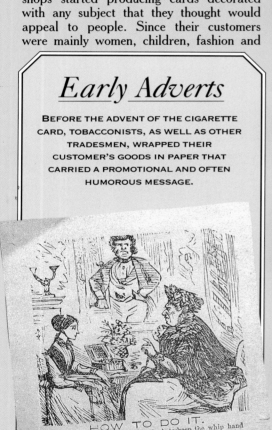

Early Adverts

BEFORE THE ADVENT OF THE CIGARETTE
CARD, TOBACCONISTS, AS WELL AS OTHER
TRADESMEN, WRAPPED THEIR
CUSTOMER'S GOODS IN PAPER THAT
CARRIED A PROMOTIONAL AND OFTEN
HUMOROUS MESSAGE.

HOW TO DO IT.

"What you've got to do, Amelia, is to keep the whip hand
of him, and if he jibs, tighten the curb. I soon tamed mine
when I took him in hand."

JOHN T. WHALEY,
TOBACCONIST.
Baker, Grocer, Tea and Provision Dealer,
Post Office, SAUGHALL.

thought of replacing the usual piece of plain cardboard in the pack with an illustrated trade card to promote their products.

In Britain, cigarette cards took a little longer to catch on, with the first sets probably appearing in the late 1880s. However, the Tobacco War (1900-1902) – a period of intense competition between American and British tobacco companies – caused a massive increase in the number of cigarette cards produced in Britain from 1901. By the start of the Edwardian period, however, the hobby of collecting the cards had become firmly established.

THE FIRST GOLDEN AGE

This boom – the first 'golden age' of *cartophily*, or cigarette-card collecting – lasted throughout Edward's reign and into World War I, until a paper shortage in 1917 put an end to the production of such

◀ *The collector interested in sports will discover a wealth of appealing subjects in Edwardian cigarette cards. One of the most popular categories of this first 'golden age' of cigarette cards was horse racing. Examples of famous horses and jockeys of the time can be found quite easily. However, less common sports, such as wrestling, may present more of a challenge.*

▲ *Although horse racing was considered a gentlemanly sport, it was not purely the preserve of the wealthy. Punters from all walks of life flocked to the racetracks. It was with this group of people in mind that many cigarette companies produced collectable sets of cards featuring the horses, the jockeys and the racing colours of the owners.*

collectable items for several years to come.

During the Edwardian period, the vast majority of smokers were men. Although the range of subjects chosen for cigarette-card sets steadily broadened, the illustrations on the earlier ones usually reflected typical male interests – beautiful women, military subjects and various sports.

British sporting cigarette cards naturally concentrated on the most popular games in the country, around 70 per cent of such sets issued in the Edwardian period covering football or cricket. Sets connected with racing and other riding events came a poor third, accounting for only about 10 per cent of British sporting sets issued during this period. This, however, is still about three times as many as were issued for each of the next most popular sports – boxing and golf. Other sporting subjects that had little

popularity when issued are now highly prized. For example, one of only a few cigarette companies to issue a set devoted to wrestling during this period was the British firm Taddy, and there were only two cards in this now rare and valuable set.

Besides those previously mentioned, the sports covered on British cards include polo, athletics, coursing, swimming, fishing, ju jitsu and billiards. On cards issued by American cigarette companies, baseball is by far the most featured sport.

Although most series were devoted to one particular sport, some covered a wide range, often including obscure pursuits of limited appeal such as the techniques of tent pegging and otter hunting.

NOVELTY CARDS

Most cigarette cards are about $2\frac{1}{2} \times 1\frac{1}{4}$ inches (6.4cm × 3.2cm) in size, but there are many exceptions. A few were smaller, and there is a range of larger sizes going up to the (then) standard postcard size of $5\frac{1}{2} \times 3\frac{1}{2}$ inches (14cm × 9cm) and beyond. But not all were made in a rectangular form and, while still referred to as cards, some were made from other materials, such as plastic, metal, and various fabrics, notably silk. Such items are called novelty cards, a broad category that even includes cards with miniature gramophone records on one side. Examples of novelty cards in the sporting category include the 1901 sets of small, circular celluloid 'buttons' produced by the American Tobacco Company that depicted cricketers and jockeys. These items had pins on the back, and could be worn as badges or fixed to a special souvenir card.

Horses and Riders

Of all the cigarette cards featuring horses and riders, the most popular are those connected with racing. A few show races in progress, but such scenes are generally quite detailed and, therefore, not ideal subjects for reproduction on a small card. So most racing cards show winning horses, famous jockeys or, sometimes, both.

Cards entitled 'Horses of Today', issued in 1906 by Wills for Capstan, Vice Regal and Havelock cigarettes, show jockeys sitting on racehorses in rural settings. On the back of each card are details of the horse, including its breeding, age and racecourse successes. Other sets depict similar scenes, but with the jockeys standing beside the horses.

Ogden's 1906 set of 50 cards of 'Owners Racing Colours and Jockeys' shows close-ups of jockeys in the racing colours of the owners for whom they rode. In a 1914 25-card set of the same name (but with a comma after the word 'owners'), each card shows a portrait of the owner alongside the jockey.

Many other riding sports appear on cigarette cards, including polo, a sport which originated in the East and was often played by the British living in India.

◀ *Jockey Otto Madden, dressed in the red and yellow colours of G.A. Prentice, is part of Ogden's set of 50 racing cards.*

PRICE GUIDE ③

▲ *Ogden's 'Racehorses' series included 50 great horses. Prince Bathyany's chestnut brown Galopin is part of the set.*

PRICE GUIDE ③

PRICE GUIDE REFERS TO SETS OF CARDS, NOT SINGLES.

▼ *Gorgos was tipped, on the reverse of this card, to become a big star. Part of a set of 50.*

PRICE GUIDE ③

▶ *L. H. Hewitt is one of the men featured in Taddy & Co's set of 25 'Famous Jockeys' cards.*

PRICE GUIDE ⑥

PRICE GUIDE

▶ White Eagle, *a powerful horse of the early 1900s, is part of a set of 25 issued by Job Cigarettes.*

PRICE GUIDE **5**

▼ *A jockey sits astride one of the King's horses, Minoru, on another card from Job's series of 25 famous horses.*

PRICE GUIDE **5**

▼ *The yellow and lavender colours of Mr J.C. Sullivan are worn by the jockey W. Higgs. This card is included in Ogden's first set of 50 'Owners Racing Colours and Jockeys' series issued in 1906.*

PRICE GUIDE **3**

W. HIGGS.

◀▼ *Like the other jockeys in the Taddy and Co series of 25, W. Earl's portrait has been framed in a locket-shaped design.*

PRICE GUIDE **6**

▼ *Mr W. Raphael and his jockey, both feature on this card from Ogden's second, set of 25 'Owners, Racing Colours and Jockeys'.*

PRICE GUIDE **3**

FAMOUS JOCKEYS.

W.EARL.

W. SAXBY   MR. W. RAPHAEL

PRICE GUIDE

Cricket, Football and Other Sports

I n the main sport categories — football and cricket — players from various teams were featured in each set of cards, as these had to appeal to people in different parts of the country.

Many people interested in collecting whole sets of footballers prefer the coloured art cards to the black-and-white photographic types so that they can see the colours of the various teams featured. Such cards issued during the Edwardian period include Ogden's 1908 set of close-ups of 50 Famous Footballers. For fans attending matches, Ogden's produced novelty cards in eye-catching team colours with a tapering

design to be worn in a button-hole or on a hat.

Several sets showing close-ups of cricketers were produced during this period, notably by Taddy and Wills. The Wills's 1903 Australian issue of cricketers in action wrongly shows the well-known bowler E. Jones using his left arm.

Many other types of sports appeared on Edwardian cigarette cards, but the less popular ones may be found on only a small number of cards in mixed sporting sets. Few cards were issued on tennis or cycling during this period, although these sports became more popular in later years.

PRICE GUIDE REFERS TO SETS OF CARDS, NOT SINGLES.

▶ *Number six of Wills's 'Fish and Bait' set of 50 features the silver-scaled salmon and the Jock Scott fly. The reverse of the card gives information about the salmon, and a few fishing tips.*

PRICE GUIDE 1

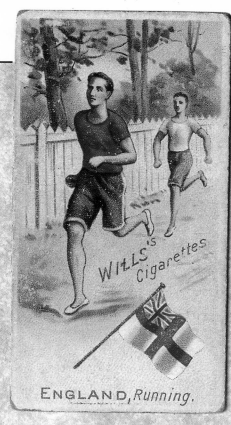

◀ *These two figures running past a white picket fence are part of England's running team, the subject of the 27th card in Wills's 'Sports of All Nations' series of 50.*

PRICE GUIDE 5

▶ *The same set also featured the mustachioed cricketer, Mr A.C. Maclaren, a well-known player at the turn of the century who held the record for the highest score made in first-class cricket. He wears the Lancashire emblem on his cap.*

PRICE GUIDE 5

◀ *J. Lumley of Brighton and Hove Albion is one of the sportsmen included in Taddy's & Co's 'Prominent Footballers' set of 595. The back of the card promotes Taddy's 'ripe, full flavoured pipe tobacco'.*

PRICE GUIDE 8

▼ *A colourful hunting scene with hounds, horses and riders is number 37 in the 'Sports of All Nations' series of 50, printed by Wills's Cigarettes in 1901.*

PRICE GUIDE 5

PRICE GUIDE

WILL'S CIGARETTES.

MR. A. C. MacLAREN (LANCS.).

WILL'S CIGARETTES.

MR. P. F. WARNER (MIDDLESEX).

◀ 'Plum' Warner, captain of the victorious team against Australia in 1903 is second in the 'Cricketers' series of 50 by Wills's Cigarettes.

PRICE GUIDE **5**

▼ The 'How to Keep Fit' exercise number 22, printed by Drapkin's Cigarettes, instructed the Edwardian man on how to develop the muscles of the upper and lower arms. Part of a set of 25.

PRICE GUIDE **5**

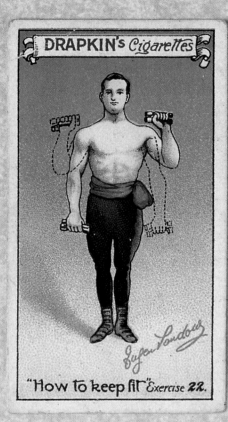

DRAPKIN's Cigarettes

"How to keep fit" Exercise 22.

WILL'S Cigarettes. ENGLAND, BOWLS.

◀ Number eight in Wills's 'Sports of All Nations' set of 50 is the classic English outdoor game of bowls.

PRICE GUIDE **5**

COPE'S

DIXIE KID

CIGARETTES

LAMBERT & BUTLER'S CIGARETTES,

SKI-ING, THE TELEMARK TURN.

◀ The American Aaron L. Brown, better known as the Dixie Kid, is number 11 in Cope's 'Boxers' run of 25. His career details are listed on the back.

PRICE GUIDE **3**

▲ Number 10 out of a set of 25 'Winter Sports' by Lambert and Butler's, instructs skiers on when and how to perform the difficult telemark turn.

PRICE GUIDE **3**

PRICE GUIDE

◄ COLLECTOR'S TIPS ►

Although cigarette cards are collected for many reasons, nostalgia accounts for their appeal to some older collectors, who probably used them to play card games during their schooldays. Since these games usually involved flicking the cards in one way or another, examples that have undergone such treatment usually have little value because of their dirty condition and the damage to the corners and edges unless, of course, they are extremely rare and valuable items.

Fortunately there have been serious collectors from early on who valued the cards for their looks, or because of interest in one or more of the many subjects depicted on them. Such collectors usually treasured their cards and stored them carefully in albums, so most sets, even many of the early ones, are still available in good or even mint condition today.

The backs of many early Edwardian cards had ornate designs incorporating the tobacco company's name and, sometimes, the brand of cigarettes with which the cards were issued. Other series were more informative, with most of the space on the backs being devoted to details of the subject on the front. These are of special appeal since an album of such cards forms, in effect, an informative illustrated book.

ALBUMS AND FRAMES

In addition to the cards, cigarette companies also issued albums in which to store the sets. Once the cards were mounted in an album, their backs could not be seen, so any information printed there was generally repeated in the album, alongside the spaces reserved for the cards.

Although some collectors today are happy to keep sets of cards in their original albums, most prefer to store them in modern albums with clear plastic pages that protect the cards and allow the backs to be seen as well as the fronts.

Alternatively, sets or other groups of cards may be framed for display on a wall. It is more economical to do the framing yourself, using a kit purchased from one of the major cigarette card dealers. The frames come in several sizes, with mounts ready cut to take various numbers and sizes of cards. The mounts are designed to hold the cards without causing damage, and the frames are glazed on both sides so that the backs of the cards can be inspected.

CARD PRICES

The interest in collecting cigarette cards has grown steadily in recent years, and the increased demand has forced up prices. Some people who started collecting purely because they liked the cards have now diverted large amounts of their savings into this field, hoping prices will continue to rise.

◄ COMPARISONS ►

Borderline

ALTHOUGH THESE TWO TADDY & CO CARDS APPEAR VERY SIMILAR, THE LEFT-HAND ONE WITHOUT THE THIN GOLD BORDER IS RARER AND FAR MORE VALUABLE THAN THE OTHER ONE.

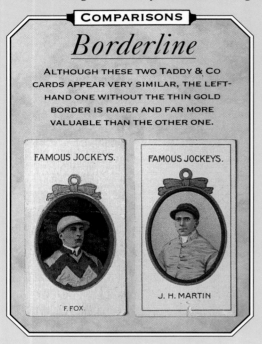

FAMOUS JOCKEYS.   FAMOUS JOCKEYS.

F. FOX.   J. H. MARTIN.

A Derby Day Panorama

IN 1914, THE FIRM OF W.D. & H.O. WILLS INCLUDED IN THEIR PACKS OF SCISSORS CIGARETTES, A 25-PIECE SET OF CARDS. THESE CARDS, WHEN CORRECTLY PIECED TOGETHER, FORMED A COMPLETE PANORAMA OF THE DERBY DAY EVENTS AT THE EPSOM RACECOURSE IN SURREY, THE GREATEST RACING OCCASION OF THE YEAR.

THE PANORAMA DEPICTED A LIVELY SCENE IN WHICH PLEBEIANS AND PATRICIANS MINGLED, UNITED BY A COMMON ENTHUSIASM FOR THE TURF. BOTH CLASSES DRESSED IN THEIR FINEST CLOTHES, FOR THIS WAS A SOCIAL AS WELL AS A RACING EVENT.

VIBRANT CHROMOLITHOGRAPHIC PRINTING PICTURED THE IMPRESSIVE GRANDSTAND, THE PADDOCK AND THE VARIOUS CROWDED ENCLOSURES, AS WELL AS HORSES AND RIDERS.

FOUR OUT OF THE 25 CARDS ARE SHOWN BELOW. THESE INCLUDE NUMBERS 6, 8, 11 AND 16. NUMBERS 6 AND 11 FIT TOGETHER TO FORM A VIEW OF THE GRANDSTAND AND THE OTHER TWO SHOW DIFFERENT FRAGMENTS OF THE PICTURE.

① THERE IS NOTICEABLE DAMAGE TO THE EDGES OF THE CARDS.

② BRIGHT COLOURS PRODUCED BY CHROMOLITHOGRAPHY.

③ TWO CARDS JOIN TOGETHER TO FORM A SMALL SECTION OF THE SCENE.

CLOSE UP

① DAMAGED CORNER

OWNERS RACING COLOURS & JOCKEYS

A SERIES OF 50

② SERIES TITLE

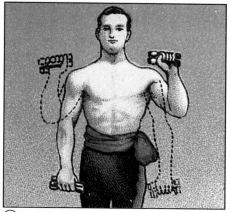

③ INSTRUCTIVE CARD

JOB CIGARETTES

④ COMPANY NAME

CRICKETERS
4
WILL'S CIGARETTES

Mr. A. C. Maclaren.

(Harrow—Lancashire—England.)

⑤ SERIES INFORMATION

Jock Scott

⑥ INSET

① THE DAMAGE TO THE LOWER RIGHT CORNER OF THIS CARD CONSIDERABLY REDUCES ITS VALUE.

④ THE NAME OF THE ISSUING COMPANY, JOB CIGARETTES, IS CLEARLY OUTLINED.

② THE ABSENCE OF A COMMA IN THE TITLE DENOTES A CARD FROM THE FIRST (1906) RUN OF THIS OGDEN'S SERIES.

⑤ THE BACK OF THE CARD GIVES DETAILS OF THE SERIES AND THE COMPANY NAME.

③ THE EXERCISE MAN ILLUSTRATES HOW TO BUILD UP MUSCLES, WITH DUMBELLS, IN THE LOWER AND UPPER ARMS.

⑥ THIS CARD HIGHLIGHTS THE CORRECT FLY TO USE TO CATCH SALMON

Sport is one of the most popular themes collected, and some of the rarer cards have seen some spectacular price rises in recent times. For example, the Ogden's Golf series issued in 1901 now fetches about £180 for a set of 18 cards in a good, clean condition and, as with all cards of this period, about double that amount for a mint set. But these are cheap compared with the postcard-size golfing cigarette cards issued by Felix S Berlyn in 1910, which now cost £200 each in good condition.

One of the most important factors determining the price of cigarette cards is their condition. The first and last cards of a set which has been stored in numerical order in a wad held together by an elastic band often become damaged. The elastic may cut into the end cards, or stick to them as it ages and perishes, and these vulnerable cards are also handled more often. For this reason, the first and last cards in a series are generally more difficult to find in good condition and, being scarcer, cost more.

POINTS TO WATCH

■ Damaged cards have little value, although the subject matter may still appeal. If you buy such cards to cut cost, you may find it difficult to find a buyer, should you ever wish to sell.

■ If you are offered an apparently rare card at a bargain price, beware – it could be a modern reprint of little value. Look for a 'reprint' warning on the back, or any sign that one may have been removed.

■ Do not buy a card just because you notice an error on it and hope that this may make it valuable. Wrong captions or spelling mistakes are regarded merely as interesting oddities and, unlike errors on postage stamps, do not necessarily command a premium.

■ Store your cards carefully in frames or albums that guard against damage.

▶ *Wills's collectable billiard series of 1909 illustrates and explains the techniques of difficult and trick shots.*

WILLS'S CIGARETTES.

Cups and Trophies

The shape and design of sporting trophies, especially those connected with equestrian events, have followed the changing fashions in metalware over the centuries

Trophies in the form of plates or cups have been presented to the owners of the winning horses in races since the days of Charles II. Made from silver, silver-gilt or gold and varying in shape and design, the trophies made for top racing events, such as the most important flat races and steeplechases of the season, were often very elaborate.

RACING BELLS

The first racecourse was established in the reign of Henry VIII on the Roodee at Chester in 1540. There was an annual prize which took the form of a silver or gold bell, which was almost spherical in shape with a ring in the top. Examples survive from the late 16th century, an interesting one being a pair of racing bells with the date 1599 inscribed, bearing the inscription 'The sweftes horse thes bel to tak for mi Lade Daker sake.' The Lady Dacre referred to was probably the wife of William Lord Dacre, the governor of Carlisle under Elizabeth I.

By the time of James I cups had been adopted as prizes. The King was a keen follower of the Turf, as were all his Stuart successors, and he added new stables and a grandstand on the Heath at Newmarket. Charles I established regular meetings in the spring and autumn at Newmarket, and instituted the Newmarket Gold Cup in 1634.

CUPS AND PLATES

During the reign of Charles II it became normal to offer a considerable piece of silver or gold in the form of a plate or cup as first prize. This might also be used as a container for a 'purse' – a sum of prize money – which added to the value of the prize. From these early times the trophy was given as a genuine, rather than a symbolic prize, and was kept by the winning owner rather than being returned and given to the new winner the following year.

Few of these early trophies survive, the Frampton Moor Cup of 1666 being perhaps the earliest, although from the 18th century there are many more examples. Queen Anne presented a number of gold and silver cups, including one particularly memorable example in gold made in 1705 by Pierre Harache for a race at Richmond in Yorkshire, which cost the princely sum of £122 14s 3d.

Another interesting cup surviving from the early 18th century is a simple two-handled gold cup engraved with a picture of a rider on a racing horse and the words 'Won at York ye 5 of August 1725 by Cuthbert Routh Esq.' However, at this time many other silver objects were presented as racing prizes. Punch bowls were common; a pair of double-lipped sauce boats were the trophy at Rapston,

Hertfordshire in 1729. Salvers were also used, even a silver snuff box in the shape of a horse's hoof complete with racing 'plate' and with a lid engraved with two horses and their jockeys at a full gallop was given as a trophy.

TEAPOT TROPHIES

Teapots were also offered. Gold teapots were made in Edinburgh to be presented for The King's Plate, run at Leith in Midlothian in 1736 and 1737. An English silver teapot inscribed 'Well Ridden Miriam Wrighton. Spott. Rippon 1723' and engraved with a lady riding side-saddle was presented with a silver tea caddy for a race between nine 'gentlewomen riders', which is said to have scandalized the entire neighbourhood.

An Act of 1740 decreed that no event could be worth less than £50 to the winner. The money for these trophies and cash prizes was raised from the owners themselves in the form of stakes and forfeits.

126

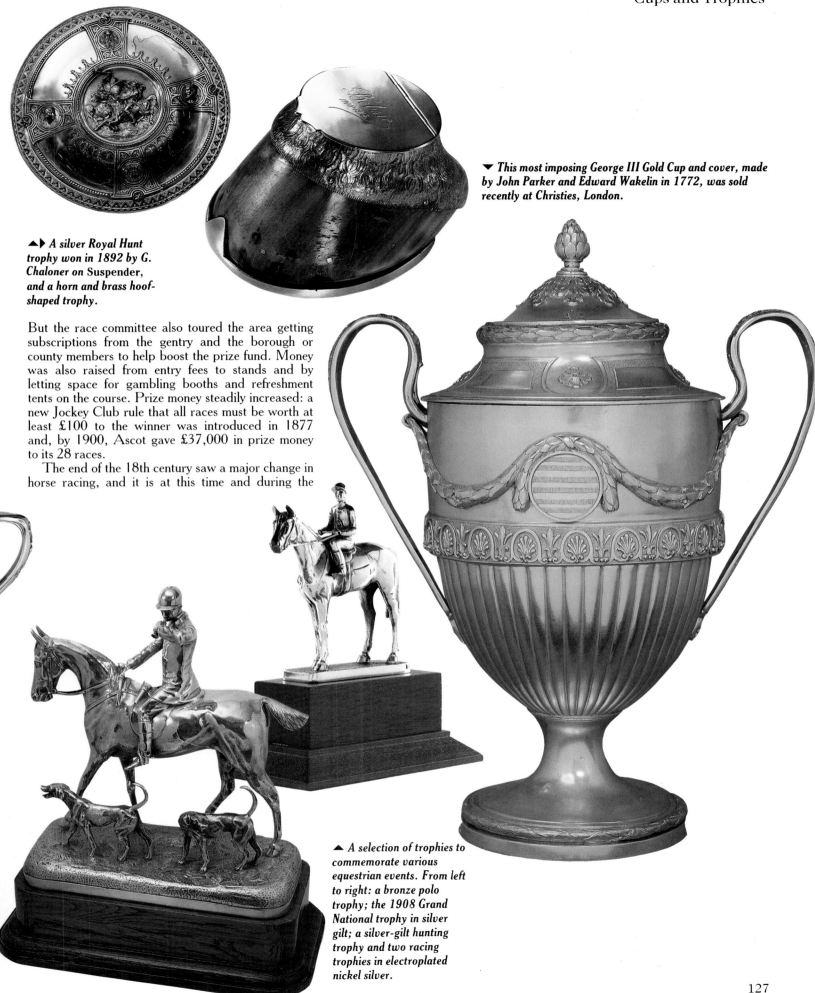

A silver Royal Hunt trophy won in 1892 by G. Chaloner on Suspender, and a horn and brass hoof-shaped trophy.

▼ *This most imposing George III Gold Cup and cover, made by John Parker and Edward Wakelin in 1772, was sold recently at Christies, London.*

But the race committee also toured the area getting subscriptions from the gentry and the borough or county members to help boost the prize fund. Money was also raised from entry fees to stands and by letting space for gambling booths and refreshment tents on the course. Prize money steadily increased: a new Jockey Club rule that all races must be worth at least £100 to the winner was introduced in 1877 and, by 1900, Ascot gave £37,000 in prize money to its 28 races.

The end of the 18th century saw a major change in horse racing, and it is at this time and during the

▲ *A selection of trophies to commemorate various equestrian events. From left to right: a bronze polo trophy; the 1908 Grand National trophy in silver gilt; a silver-gilt hunting trophy and two racing trophies in electroplated nickel silver.*

The King Wins the Derby. 1896.

▶ Persimmon, *owned by the Prince of Wales (later King Edward VII), and ridden by jockey Jack Watts, forged ahead in the last 100 yards to win the 1896 Derby by a head.*

▼ *Owned by the International Horse Show, this magnificent King George V Gold Cup was presented by the late King George V to be competed for by military officers of any nationality.*

▲ *This beautifully styled Addendance Cup was presented by H Eliot Walton in 1914 to the winner of the Racing Lads Sunday Class at Epsom.*

early years of the 19th century that most of the great races were inaugurated which carried the finest trophies for the winner.

From 1670 to about 1780 races were run in heats, usually four of four miles each, all completed in the same day with half an hour for a rub-down between rides. In 1776 the first important 'dash' – a two-mile race for three-year-olds – was held at Doncaster. It became the St. Leger. In 1779 the 12th Earl of Derby and his friends devised a similar sweepstake for fillies at Epsom, which was named

after his own house – The Oaks. Following this success, he added a one-and-a-half-mile race for colts during the next year, which was named after himself and became known as 'the blue ribband of the Turf' – the Derby.

These races, together with the 1,000 guineas and the 2,000 guineas at Newmarket, make up the five so-called 'Classics' of the English race-track, and magnificent cash prizes and trophies were awarded to the owners of the winning horses.

The other most important races became the cups,

▲ *Cups and trophies also abound for a variety of other sports such as fishing, running, rowing, billiards and boxing.*

such as the Royal Hunt Cup and the Gold Cup at Ascot, the Goodwood Cup, the Doncaster Cup and the Jockey Club Cup at Newmarket among others. The Epsom Cup was renamed the Coronation Cup in 1902 to celebrate the coronation of Edward VII.

An earlier and equally famous Prince of Wales who became Prince Regent and later George IV presented the Brighton Cup of 1805. This was a silver-gilt, two-handled covered urn bearing a relief of the Royal Pavilion in its early form on one side and Victory presenting a crown to the winner of a classical horse race on the other. The cup has a fret pattern encircling the rim and acanthus leaves decorating the bottom, with relief masks below the handles and a finial with a coronet of the Prince of Wales' feathers. The inscription reads 'The Brighton Cup 1805 Won by Orwill' and on the other side 'The Gift of His Highness the Prince of Wales to Chris Wilson.' This is somewhat unusual because the owner of the winning horse was actually the Prince of Wales himself. He had bought Orwill from Chris Wilson. Perhaps the cup was intended as both a thank you and a consolation prize, but at any rate it remained in the family until bought by Brighton Corporation.

The two-handled covered vase with engraving, inscription and decorated finial was the standard shape for 19th-century trophies but, as the century went on, some designs became increasingly elaborate and excessively ornate.

GOLD CUPS

Most of the so-called 'gold cups' were actually made in silver-gilt (an exception being the Ascot Gold Cup inaugurated in 1807, which is solid gold), but

decoration could be extravagant. Frosting and burnishing, parcel gilding, matting and oxidization were used to decorate the surface of the metal, and cast sculpture as well as cast and repoussé bas reliefs began to appear as decorative features.

Racing trophies turn up in general auctions of silverware as well as in antique shops, but really interesting examples and ones pertaining to famous races may be fairly few and far between. Nineteenth-century cups are the most commonly found. Of these there are some astonishing creations in sculptural silver. Scenes depicted on such cups include racing and hunting scenes, knights in armour, St. George slaying the dragon and 'The Rape of the Daughters of Leucippus'. Such decorative extravagances were mocked by workers in silverware at the turn of the century like Charles Robert Ashbee, who created a new and much simpler style which later became popular.

▼ *An Edwardian shield-shaped trophy in wood and silvered metal – a prize for a boxing tournament.*

·PRICE GUIDE· SPORTING TROPHIES

Although many fine sporting trophies remain in private collections, some of the prices achieved at auction recently show how even a small amount of good quality engraving and decoration can enhance the value of a trophy.

The Liverpool Autumn Cup of 1846, decorated on the cover with a sculptural group of armoured knights sold recently for £4,000 while the

silver-gilt Doncaster Cup of 1820 with relief work and mask and foliate handles reached £7,000.

At the other end of the scale, an 1870s rowing trophy in EPNS with a plain cup set on three upturned oars resting on a 'straw' boater would fetch up to £165, and a 1910 EPNS billiard trophy set on three cues encircled with a wreath, up to £100.

Golfing Collectables

The golfing boom of Edwardian times resulted in a wealth of equipment and memorabilia, highly sought-after by golfing enthusiasts today

I n political and social life the early years of the 20th century were a time of transition. So it was with sport and leisure, too, and the Edwardian era saw the expansion of a golfing boom which had begun during the last few decades of the 19th century. By then, it was not unusual for the enthusiastic player to own an array of golfing equipment, including several clubs and various accessories, all of which were most probably kept in the lobby of his country or town house.

GOLFING BEGINNINGS

Golf had started long before the 19th century. The game as we know it now undoubtedly grew up in Scotland, but its origins are obscure. It may have evolved from a game known as 'colf' which was played in Holland as long ago as the 14th century. In colf, a ball was struck cross country towards a set target such as a tree or building, using a club similar to today's golf club.

During the 16th and 17th centuries, there was much trade and cultural contact between Scotland and the Low Countries, and it is quite possible that early Scottish club-and-ball games evolved at this time, with some influence from colf, into what we now know as the game of golf.

The first mention of golf in Scotland was in a Royal Decree of 1457, when James II forbade the playing of football and golf. Apparently, these sports were keeping the young men from their archery practice, essential in the defence of the kingdom. The fact that a Royal Decree had to be issued to curtail the playing of golf suggests that the game was already popular at the time.

Mary, Queen of Scots, was said to be especially fond of the game and when, in 1603, her son James VI of Scotland became James I of England, he brought his golf clubs as well as his court to London. James' son, Henry played golf on the rough land by the Thames at Greenwich – the land that was to become the Royal Blackheath Golf Club in 1608.

Over the next 200 years, the game grew gradually in popularity. In 1754 the Royal and Ancient Golf Club of St Andrews was formed, and it was here that it was established that 18 holes should be standard for a golf course.

COMPARISONS

Early Clubs

METAL-HEADED 'IRONS' WITH HICKORY SHAFTS, SUCH AS THIS EXAMPLE, CAME INTO USE IN THE EARLY 1800S. THESE BECAME INCREASINGLY POPULAR THROUGHOUT THE CENTURY SINCE THEY LEFT THE NEW GUTTA-PERCHA BALLS RELATIVELY UNDAMAGED.

At this time, the game was mainly restricted to the wealthy, largely because the balls were so expensive. They were made of leather which was stuffed with a boiled feather mixture. Each ball could cost up to three times as much as a club, and obviously did not last long when struck hard, especially in wet conditions.

THE GOLFING EXPLOSION

The cost and popularity of the 'Royal and Ancient' game changed dramatically in the middle of the 19th century. The middle classes were beginning to enjoy increasing income and leisure time. Their adoption of golf was greatly aided by the introduction of the gutta-percha ball in 1848. Gutta-percha is a resin from a Malaysian tree, and golf balls made from it proved to be both durable and waterproof. They were also cheap, and this helped set in motion the golfing explosion. In 1870 there were about 30 golf clubs in the United Kingdom; by 1890 the number had increased to over 300, and by about 1905 there were some 3000 clubs.

The first British championship was held in Prestwick, Scotland, in 1860; eight

◀ Kitted out in flat tweed cap, knickerbockers and tie, the Edwardian golfer's dress was eminently practical on links exposed to wind.

professionals competed for a leather challenge belt. In the following year, both amateurs and professionals competed in the first Open Championship. In 1863, £5 prize money was awarded to the winner; by 1880 this had become £20 and by the turn of the century over £100. These were not huge prizes, even in those days, and the era of big money was yet to come. The professionals – a growing band in Edwardian times – supplemented any tournament wins they had by taking wagers on games, as well as giving instructions on techniques and selling golfing equipment.

EQUIPMENT AND MEMENTOES

With the gutta-percha ball and the rubber-cored Haskell ball which appeared at the start of the 20th century, golf balls had undergone great changes. Clubs progressed at a more leisurely pace. During the 19th century there had been various refinements in shape and construction, and an increasing use of iron-headed clubs, which did not destroy the gutta-percha balls, as they did the 'featheries'.

By Edwardian times clubs could be purchased relatively cheaply, since they were virtually mass-produced. A few club-makers were still at work producing superb articles by hand, as they had done until the beginning of the century.

▲ This charming picture of St Andrews golf course shows that Edwardian Scots, like their earlier and modern-day compatriots, managed to enjoy the game, even when they had to play a ball from the sand trap.

As golf entered the popular imagination, its influence spread into other realms. Songs and books were written about the game, golfing cartoons were drawn, and silver and porcelain mementoes were made. Golf had truly arrived.

Today, golfing mementoes are much sought-after, though the pleasure of collecting them need not coincide with a passion for playing the links. For those infected with the golfing bug, there is no better way to get involved with the history of the game than by collecting some of its artefacts. A wise and still reasonably affordable investment can be clubs, plates, figurines or pictures. Once displayed, they make good conversation pieces.

An absorbing hobby, golf collecting is enjoyable. To promote the pleasure of collecting, and to allow the exchange of information between members, a golf collectors' society was formed in 1970. Membership is now spread over 19 different countries and there is an annual meeting in the United States as well as one held sometime during the British Open.

Golfing Memorabilia

Edwardian golfing enthusiasts did not need to be away from golf when they were off the golf course. Tea could be taken from a Royal Doulton tea set decorated with golfing figures, and after tea a golfing book like Mrs Edward Kennard's *The Golf Lunatic and his Cycling Wife*, C R Bauchope's *Golfing Annual* or the Rev. T D Miller's *Famous Scottish Links* could be browsed at leisure.

Magazines like *Punch, The Illustrated London News* and *Vanity Fair* regularly ran articles on golf and printed cartoons and engravings illustrating the game, often humorously. A multitude of golfing books were published early this century.

Watercolours and oil paintings on golfing themes were popular, and golf was represented in silver, glass and ceramic ware.

Particularly attractive are golfing desk sets. These usually consist of a central figure standing in a golfing pose, flanked by inkwells which are sometimes in the shape of golf balls.

Cigarette cases, clocks and sets of coffee spoons and cocktail sticks were decorated with golfing motifs, as were hatpins, cigarette lighters and ashtrays. Statuettes in bronze or silver were great favourites and often featured great golfers of the time like Harry Vardon, John Henry Taylor and James Braid; these three are known as the Great Triumvirate and between them they won most of the British Opens between 1894 and 1914.

And there are medals and trophies, often presented to the winners of competitions, for victory in the smallest tournament was regarded then, as it is today, as well worth commemorating.

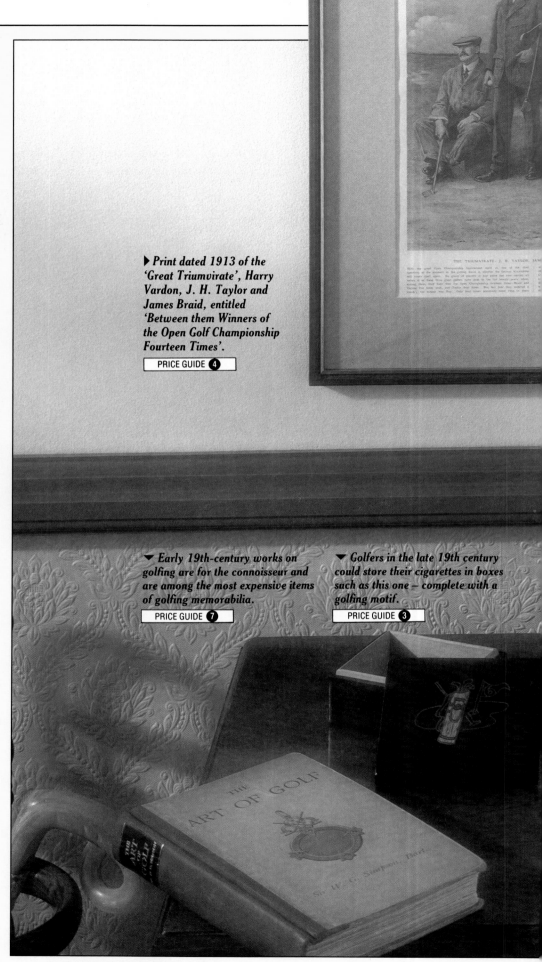

▶ *Print dated 1913 of the 'Great Triumvirate', Harry Vardon, J. H. Taylor and James Braid, entitled 'Between them Winners of the Open Golf Championship Fourteen Times'.*

PRICE GUIDE **4**

▼ *Early 19th-century works on golfing are for the connoisseur and are among the most expensive items of golfing memorabilia.*

PRICE GUIDE **7**

▼ *Golfers in the late 19th century could store their cigarettes in boxes such as this one – complete with a golfing motif.*

PRICE GUIDE **3**

PRICE GUIDE

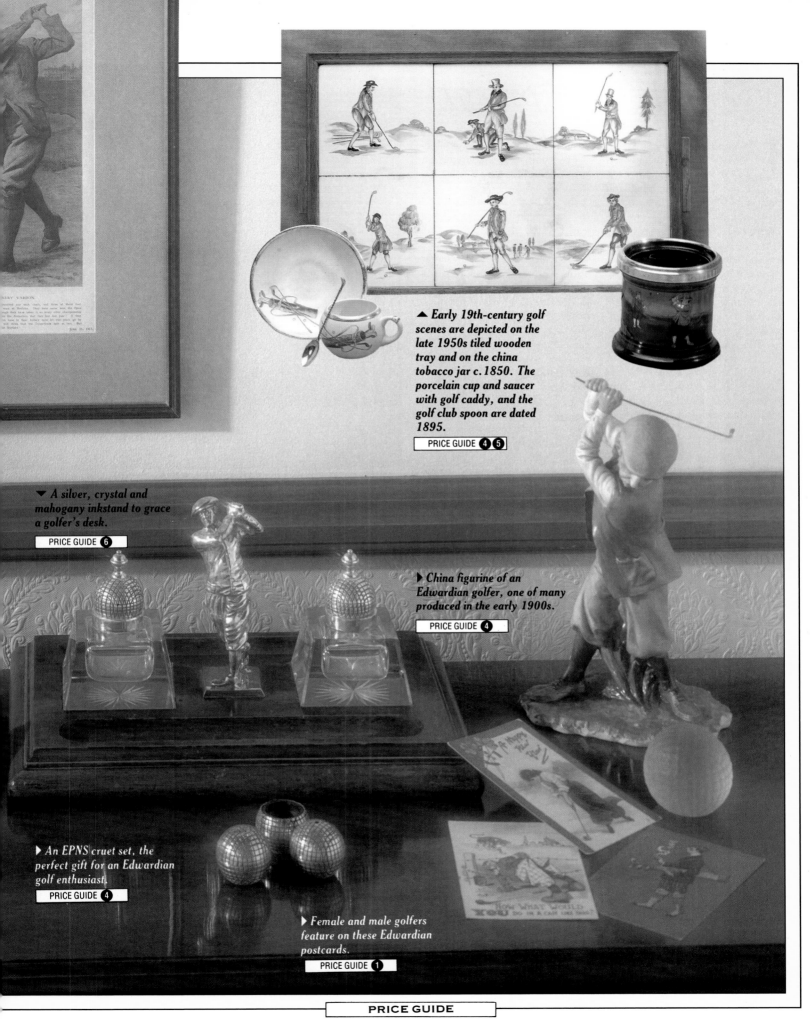

▲ **Early 19th-century golf scenes are depicted on the late 1950s tiled wooden tray and on the china tobacco jar c. 1850. The porcelain cup and saucer with golf caddy, and the golf club spoon are dated 1895.**

PRICE GUIDE **4** **5**

▼ *A silver, crystal and mahogany inkstand to grace a golfer's desk.*

PRICE GUIDE **6**

▶ *China figurine of an Edwardian golfer, one of many produced in the early 1900s.*

PRICE GUIDE **4**

▶ *An EPNS cruet set, the perfect gift for an Edwardian golf enthusiast.*

PRICE GUIDE **4**

▶ *Female and male golfers feature on these Edwardian postcards.*

PRICE GUIDE **1**

PRICE GUIDE

Golfing Equipment

Everyday clothes, hobnail boots and a bright red coat – to warn the public of the danger of flying golf balls – had been the golfer's costume in the days before organized golf courses. By Edwardian times, knickerbockers had come into vogue, as had Norfolk jackets, which gave plenty of room for the swing. A flat golfing cap was often favoured. The ladies, too, wore practical clothes — loose blouses and long skirts to allow a full and fluid action.

Clubs were wooden or metal headed. American hickory had become the dominant material for shafts, and remained so until sheet shafts were approved in the late 1920s. Wooden heads were of yet another American wood – persimmon.

Iron-headed clubs had become increasingly important with the demise of the feather-stuffed ball, and aluminium and brass-headed putters were also popular.

In 1900 a new ball appeared to supersede the gutta-percha ball – the Haskell. A long narrow strip of rubber was wound around a central core and surrounded by a gutta-percha covering. This ball was as durable as its predecessor but softer, so it did not damage club faces. Most modern balls are similar in design to the Haskell.

Thus equipped, the golfer was ready for a game. All that remained was the golf bag, which had recently come into vogue. These 'automatic caddies' were of leather or canvas on a wooden frame, and were most welcome, as golfer or caddy had, up till then, to carry the cumbersome golf clubs around underarm.

▶ *Edwardian golfing trophies, made of pewter and of silver, are engraved with the details of special competitions. These affordable collectables are good conversation pieces which can be used as an attractive display.*

PRICE GUIDE **4**

▶ *Edwardian caddy bags were constructed of canvas and leather, usually around a wooden frame. This example, made in 1910, can still be used to carry clubs.*

PRICE GUIDE **3**

▼ *Three golf balls, two from the Victorian period, made of gutta-percha – an inexpensive resin – and an Edwardian white-cased rubber one.*

PRICE GUIDE **3 1**

▲ *An aluminium caddy trolley, c. 1920.*

PRICE GUIDE **6**

PRICE GUIDE

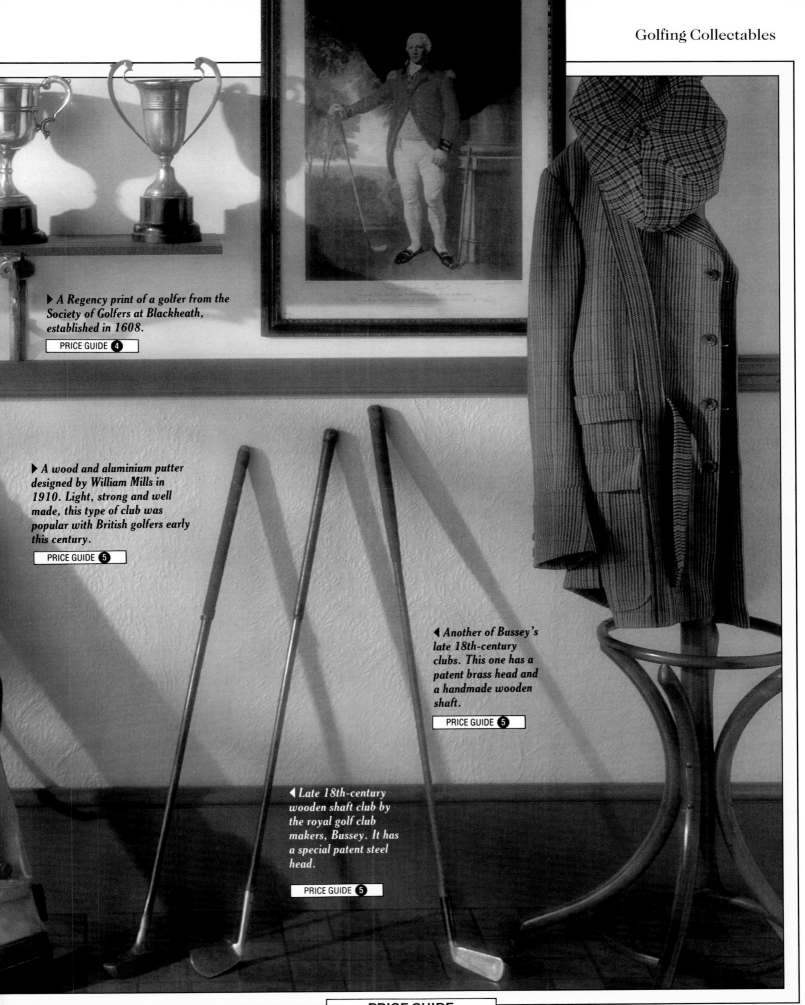

▶ *A Regency print of a golfer from the Society of Golfers at Blackheath, established in 1608.*

PRICE GUIDE **4**

▶ *A wood and aluminium putter designed by William Mills in 1910. Light, strong and well made, this type of club was popular with British golfers early this century.*

PRICE GUIDE **5**

◀ *Another of Bussey's late 18th-century clubs. This one has a patent brass head and a handmade wooden shaft.*

PRICE GUIDE **5**

◀ *Late 18th-century wooden shaft club by the royal golf club makers, Bussey. It has a special patent steel head.*

PRICE GUIDE **5**

PRICE GUIDE

Although almost all golfing antiques are popular and sought-after, starting a collection, especially one based around a certain theme, should easily be within the grasp of most enthusiasts' pockets.

The most obvious golf collectables are clubs. Although 19th-century ones are now expensive, those from the early years of this century are less so. In contrast to the handmade clubs of earlier times, Edwardian wooden clubs were virtually mass-produced, whilst iron heads were forged.

Mass-produced clubs were numbered for the benefit of the golfer, telling him, for example, the degree of lift the club would impart to the ball. Thus the club names used by the Victorians and Edwardians were fated to disappear from use, but these names are part of the pleasure of collecting — look for 'mashies', 'niblicks' and 'spoons'.

There were several means of attaching wooden heads to shafts, and a complete collection should contain clubs with the older 'scared' (spliced) joints, as well as the more typically Edwardian socket joints.

During much of the 19th century there were relatively few golfers, but by the Edwardian era there were many thousands of players; each would have had about ten clubs, and many of these have survived. So ignore Edwardian clubs priced in double figures; the proper price, except in special cases, is in single figures.

Wooden heads and shafts should be inspected for undue wear and tear, and of course for woodworm; irons should be checked for excessive rust.

Golf balls are also very collectable. Feathery balls are rare and often damaged. Gutta-percha balls are easier to come by. Early 'gutties' were smooth, but when it was found that slightly battered balls flew better off the face of the club, the balls were textured, at first by hand, and then in the moulds in which they were made. An interesting little selection of golf balls, showing manufactured 'gutties' (perhaps accompanied by a mould), smooth and hand-textured gutties, an early Haskell, perhaps a modern ball and — if possible — a feathery, would be worth collecting.

Golf-associated memorabilia are legion, and the best aim is probably to go for a particular period — such as the Edwardian — or a particular theme. Books are popular and highly valuable. Many of the classic

Resin or Rubber?

IN THE 1900S, GUTTA-PERCHA BALLS (RIGHT) MADE OF TREE RESIN, WERE SUPERSEDED BY WHITE MOULDED BALLS WITH RUBBER CORES SIMILAR TO THOSE USED TODAY.

Scared Head Driver

AT THE BEGINNING OF THE 19TH CENTURY CLUB HEADS WERE MADE FROM LOCAL HARDWOODS SUCH AS APPLE, PEAR AND BOX-WOOD, USUALLY IN THE POPULAR LONG-NOSED SHAPE. WITH THE ADVENT OF HARD GUTTA-PERCHA BALLS IN 1848, BEECH, WHICH WAS MORE RESILIENT, WAS INTRODUCED AND HEADS BECAME SHORTER IN LENGTH.

EARLY SHAFTS WERE MADE FROM ASH OR HAZEL, BUT BY THE TURN OF THE CENTURY HICKORY WAS USED ALMOST EXCLUSIVELY.

THE CLUB HEAD WAS CONNECTED TO THE SHAFT BY MEANS OF A SCARED JOINT, HENCE THE

TERM 'SCARED HEAD'. THE SHAFT WAS SPLICED TO THE HEAD AND GLUED, THEN FURTHER STRENGTHENED WITH A BINDING SUCH AS FISHING LINE.

THE SCARED JOINT WAS REPLACED BY THE SOCKET METHOD OF JOINTING AT THE TURN OF THE CENTURY.

① HANDMADE, MID-VICTORIAN WOODEN HEAD

② SCARED-HEAD JOINT

③ BINDING TO REINFORCE JOIN OF HEAD TO SHAFT

④ HICKORY WOOD SHAFT

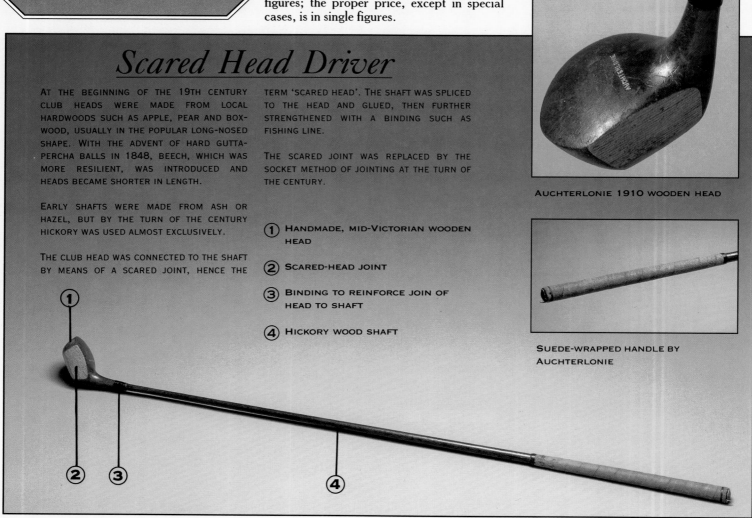

AUCHTERLONIE 1910 WOODEN HEAD

SUEDE-WRAPPED HANDLE BY AUCHTERLONIE

① ALUMINIUM HEAD

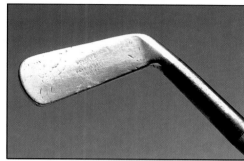

② ANTI-SHANK IRON

① WILLIAM MILLS DESIGNED THIS 1910 ALUMINIUM-HEAD PUTTER. THE BLUNT, WEDGE-SHAPED SIDE IS TEXTURED FOR BETTER CONTACT WITH THE BALL.

② THE SMOOTH-FACED, ANTI-SHANK HEAD WAS DESIGNED WITH AN 'S' SHAPE TO PREVENT THE GOLFER HITTING THE BALL SO IT WOULD FLY OFF AT AN ANGLE.

③ A PATENT STEEL SOCKET HEAD MADE BY BUSSEY & CO., LONDON, DURING THE LATTER YEARS OF THE 19TH-CENTURY, ATTACHED TO A WOODEN SHAFT.

④ A MASHIE CLUB WHICH IS USED FOR OBTAINING HEIGHT WHEN HITTING THE BALL. THIS 1920 EXAMPLE IS MADE OF HAND-FORGED STEEL.

③ PATENT STEEL HEAD

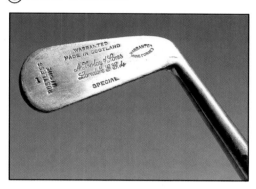

④ MASHIE HEAD

Golfing China

PORCELAIN CUP DECORATED WITH A CADDIE AND CLUBS. MADE IN THE LATE 19TH CENTURY, IT WOULD HAVE BEEN PRESENTED WITH A MATCHING SAUCER AS A GOLFING MEMENTO.

A LATE VICTORIAN MATCH STRIKER SHOWING THREE GOLFERS PLAYING A HOLE. ITS VALUE IS INCREASED BY THE FACT THAT IT IS A MARKED EXAMPLE OF CARLTON WEAR.

golf books of the early 19th century are fairly rare and expensive. Simpson's *The Art of Golf* is one. Prices for copies of Edwardian classics can go into three figures, but it is possible to pick up attractive old golf books in second-hand shops for smaller sums.

Postcards and cigarette cards on golfing themes are affordable collectables, although by no means as cheap as they once were. Golfing postcards can cost up to a few pounds each, while cigarette cards of famous golfers and golfing hints can cost somewhat more. Expect to pay quite high prices for complete sets of cigarette cards of 'Famous Golfers' or 'Golf Instruction'.

Auctions are good sources for clubs, bags and memorabilia. Some antique dealers specialize in golf; and these will be listed in antique dealers' guide books.

POINTS TO WATCH

Clubs can be easy for the unscrupulous expert to fake. Look for genuine signs of use and for genuine makers' marks.

■ Check wooden heads for woodworm, rot and excessive damage.

■ Irons may come in a poor state, thick with rust. But rust removal will not always reveal a maker's mark – the decay may have gone too far. So think before restoring.

■ If in doubt, don't buy, and try to have an expensive item authenticated. Ask the vendor whether the item has provenance – there is no better authentication for an antique club than a full history.

■ Much the same goes for other golfing antiques such as books, cigarette cases, china and so on. Ensure that they are genuine before purchase and expect to pay quite highly for items bearing golf motifs.

Early 20th-century golf tees.

The Tennis Racket

Lawn tennis was a glamorous open-air pastime that brought the sexes together. For many, a good racket and a simple outfit became passports to new social contacts

Almost every comedy set in the 1920s and 1930s includes the words 'Anyone for tennis?' They are usually spoken by a young man in blazer and white flannels who enters through the French windows and flourishes his racket before becoming distracted by a romantic situation or murder mystery.

Although its setting is upper-class (clearly there is a private court beyond the windows), this much-mocked scene does capture the sense of fun, freedom and informality that made the game so attractive during this period. In reality, tennis was no longer confined to the lawns of stately homes, but was played in parks, and in the rapidly increasing number of tennis clubs which multiplied along with the suburbs and became important social institutions. Here games could be begun without elaborate preliminary arrangements, and people of different ages could participate. An even greater advantage was that both sexes were welcome in tennis clubs, which became family establishments as well as settings for boy-meets-girl. And although the game had a distinctly middle-class character, it was open to a fairly wide public, since the required uniform of 'whites' and a racket was relatively inexpensive and easy to buy or borrow.

ORIGINS OF TENNIS

This democratization occurred late in the long history of tennis, which seems to have originated as an indoor game in medieval France. At first the player used his cupped hand to strike the ball, and the game was known as the *jeu de paume* or 'palm game'; rackets did not appear until the 15th century. French and English monarchs became enthusiastic players and the game came to be called real (meaning royal) tennis. The oldest surviving real tennis court still in use today, is that built for King Henry VIII in about 1530 at Hampton Court Palace.

These early indoor courts were extremely large (much bigger than modern tennis courts), and they required elaborate special equipment; so real tennis was never played by more than a wealthy minority. The modern outdoor game of lawn tennis developed because people with large houses and spacious grounds began to feel the need for a lawn game that was a little less sedate than croquet – though croquet literally prepared the ground for tennis, since it promoted the development of firm, well-rolled, shrub-free lawns.

▲ *A game of mixed doubles is being played at one of the new municipal tennis courts. This triptych was painted in 1932, but the men are still wearing long trousers and women sport leggings.*

▶ *This illustration from a 1922 car advertisement subtly emphasizes the fashionable and youthful image of tennis, and the social opportunities offered by the newly established tennis clubs.*

In the early 1870s, following a number of pioneer efforts, a shrewd ex-officer named Major Walter Clopton Wingfield adapted real tennis and marketed kits (including '4 tennis bats') for an outdoor game which he called Sphairistiké. This arcane title was soon dropped in favour of the simple 'lawn tennis', and the Major's hourglass-shaped court was replaced by the familiar rectangle.

THE SUCCESSFUL GAME

The new game was an overwhelming success. Feminine enthusiasm for greater physical activity was an important factor, and tennis benefited from the same social trends that produced the 'New Woman' and made cycling a symbol of emancipation. But essentially male institutions such as the universities also took the game up, and clubs were formed all over the country. In 1875 lawn tennis was introduced into the All-England Croquet Club, which became the driving force in the staging of the Wimbledon championships, first held in 1877. By this time the rules of tennis had been standarized in virtually their present-day form.

AN EDWARDIAN TENNIS RACKET WITH A 'FISH TAIL' HANDLE TO ENSURE A FIRM GRIP, AND GROOVES FOR VENTILATION.

THIS 1920S TENNIS RACKET DISPLAYS THE TRIANGULAR WEDGE OF DARK WOOD DERIVED FROM EARLY REAL TENNIS RACKETS.

A 1930S RACKET WITH INTERESTING DECORATIVE FEATURES INCLUDING A SLAZENGER SIGNATURE, AN EXOTIC 'ELTHAM' LOGO AND DISTINCTIVE COLOURED BANDS.

An important early patron was the pleasure-loving Prince of Wales (later King Edward VII), who had formerly been an exponent of real tennis. He took up the outdoor game in 1882, when he was 41, hoping that it would help him to keep down his weight. His insistence on playing at his continental haunts – Cannes, Baden-Baden and Homburg – contributed a great deal to the international popularity of this British-invented game.

By 1890 it was so well established that one observer noted, 'A lawn, a racquet, a soft ball, a net, a pot of paint, and an active member of either sex, here are all the materials needed for lawn tennis and every country house and most suburban villas can supply them'.

TENNIS STARS

Between the wars, lawn tennis also boomed as a spectator sport, a trend that necessitated moving the Wimbledon championships to larger premises. Great players such as Suzanne Lenglen and Fred Perry increasingly assumed the status of 'stars' and pin-ups adored by the young. As a result, they found themselves enrolled in the inter-war version of the Hall of Fame – the cigarette card set. Among the best-known sets featuring players' biographies were Gallaher's 'Lawn Tennis Celebrities' of 1928, Player's 1936 'Tennis', and the 1938 Ardath set issued under the same title.

Purely practical sporting considerations made tennis players pioneers of freer dress. Around 1890 lady players at Wimbledon were muttering that 15-

The smartest TENNIS OUTFIT for B·D·V coupons

RACQUET 1933 MODEL

FROCK 1933 MODEL

SHOES LATEST PATTERN

BALLS (3 IN BOX)

B·D·V FREE VOUCHER 10 COUPONS

SMOKE BDV cigarettes

▲ *Those who could not afford to pay for their tennis whites had the option of saving up their cigarette coupons instead.*

Wimbledon

THE WIMBLEDON CHAMPIONSHIPS WERE FIRST HELD IN 1877. THE ONLY COMPETITION THAT YEAR WAS THE MEN'S SINGLES, WHICH LASTED FIVE DAYS AND WAS ATTENDED BY A THOUSAND PEOPLE. THE REAL POPULARITY OF TENNIS AS A SPECTATOR SPORT DATES FROM THE EARLY 1880S, WHEN A NEW, HARD-HITTING STYLE WAS FORGED BY WIMBLEDON'S FIRST STARS, THE BROTHERS ERNEST AND WILLIAM RENSHAW. WOMEN'S SINGLES AND MEN'S DOUBLES WERE INTRODUCED IN 1884; WOMEN'S AND MIXED DOUBLES FOLLOWED AT THE TURN OF THE CENTURY. IN THE 1900S WIMBLEDON BECAME A TRULY INTERNATIONAL EVENT WHEN THE AMERICAN AND AUSTRALIAN INVASIONS BEGAN, ENDING BRITISH DOMINANCE. IN 1922 THE CHAMPIONSHIPS MOVED TO A NEW VENUE IN CHURCH STREET, WHERE THEY HAVE REMAINED EVER SINCE.

·PRICE GUIDE· TENNIS EQUIPMENT

Many items of tennis equipment survive from the inter-war years, and they are not usually expensive. Although ordinary rackets are widely available, it is worth consulting a specialist dealer for rarer items.

▼ *Although it was always a game for the elite, real tennis was still played by some in the inter-war years. This racket dates from the 1930s.*

PRICE GUIDE 5

▲▶ *The basic shape of tennis rackets may not have changed much in the 1920s and 1930s, but the presses that they were stored in came in several different styles.*

PRICE GUIDE 3

year-old Charlotte Dod had an unfair advantage because she was young enough to wear much shorter skirts than her grown-up competitors. Then, after 1900, skirt-lengths did steadily rise above the ankle, although hat-wearing women experienced difficulties since they were only able to preserve their millinery intact by serving underarm.

Much stronger shocks were in store from 1919, when the legendary Suzanne Lenglen came on to the court uncorseted, short-skirted and bare-armed, justifying the resulting freedom of action with dazzling displays of skill and agility. In a favourable social climate, thousands followed where Lenglen led, and even men's long flannel trousers began to seem cumbersome. By the late 1930s both men and women commonly wore shorts. Although the racket altered hardly at all, sport and society were interacting and changing fast.

RACKET DESIGN

The design of early lawn tennis rackets was strongly influenced by the appearance of those used in real tennis. These had long shafts and heads that were not oval but curved away to one side to make it easier for the real tennis player to scoop up and control the relatively heavy ball. An alternative design – with a head that was flattened at the end – was far longer lived, although it had disappeared by the 1920s. However, other interesting features persisted, notably the curiously designed 'fish-tail' butt, shaped to give a surer grip, the dark triangular wedge of wood inserted at the base of the head, and the double main – a set of extra strings strung across the centre of the mesh in order to strengthen it.

Up until the 1930s, tennis racket frames were made from steam bent rendered ash, but this method of manufacture gradually gave way to a new process involving the bonding together of strips of different laminated woods, which gave the racket additional strength. Steel and aluminium frames were also made in the 1930s, but they failed to catch on at that date, and did not pass into general use until their reintroduction in the 1960s.

The earliest rackets had uncovered wooden handles, but leather grips became more popular after the turn of the century, and were universal by the 1930s. Some rackets had additional gadgets such as scoring mechanisms in their handles and ways of adjusting the tension of the strings, but these unusual gimmicks never became widespread.

Strings were made from 'catgut' until cheaper modern nylon versions began to replace them. Catgut strings are actually made from sheep's intestines, and have nothing to do with cats. The name arose from a corruption of 'kit' – the word used to denote a violin in the 17th century – as the gut used to make early rackets was adapted from that found in stringed instruments.

The racket has never been completely standardized, but by the 1930s most players owned examples that were similar in general appearance. However, the workmanship, the amount of mahogany or walnut veneer and inlay on the wooden parts, and the brand name, greatly influenced price and prestige.

▲ WIMBLEDON GAVE PUBLICITY TO A NEW GENERATION OF TENNIS STARS, SUCH AS FRED PERRY, SEEN HERE ON THE LEFT, FOLLOWING THE 1931 MEN'S SINGLES SEMI-FINALS.

◀ CENTRE COURT CAPTURED THE PUBLIC IMAGINATION AND DREW IN THE CROWDS IN THE 1930s AS IT CONTINUES TO DO TODAY.

▲ Table badminton proved popular because it could be played indoors in any weather. In early badminton sets rackets came complete with presses and shuttlecocks had real feather flights.

PRICE GUIDE 4

▶ This sturdy wooden press keeps two 1930s badminton rackets in excellent shape for play.

PRICE GUIDE 5

INDEX

PICTURE CREDITS

Arcaid/Lucinda Lambton: 8/9. Steve Bisgrove: 18, 18/19, 20/1 & 22/3 guns supplied by courtesy of Holland & Holland Ltd, 24/5, 40/1, 42/3, 44/5, 47(b), 118(bl), 118/9, 120/1, 122/3, 124/5, 126/7, 128(bl), 129. Bridgeman Art Library: 10(t), 14/5, 16(tl), 17(br), 19, 35(bc), 38(bl), 49, 71(t), 74(tr), 86(b), 88/9, 90/1, 94(t) Musée de Ille de France, Sceaux/Giraudon, 116(t), Galeria d'Arte Moderna, Rome, 127, 138/9(t) City of Bristol Museum & Art Gallery © The Estate of Eric Ravilious, all rights reserved DACS 1990, Christies Colour Library: 12(t). Ray Duns: 7(t), 11(b), 12(b), 13(b), 15, 16, 17, 26, 27, 36/7, 78/9, 80/1, 82, 85(t), 87, 88, 99, 89, 90, 91, 93, 94/5, 105(br), 106/7, 115(r), 116/7, 140/1. Mary Evans Picture Library: 68(b), 70, 92, 92/3, 108/9, 117(t), 131. Fine Art Photographic Library: 4/5, 34, 35(t), 38/9, 38(br), 39(t, c, b), 85 (c,b), 86(t). Melvin Gray: 26(r), 28/9, 30/1, 32/3. Richard Green Gallery: 68(t), 84(t). Hulton Deutsch Collection: 11(t), 97, 128(r), 141. Ranald Mackechnie: 76/7, 132/3, 134/5, 136/7. Mansell Collection: 104, 104/5, 119, 128(tl). Michael Michaels: 96, 96/7, 98/9, 100/1, 102/3. Pat Morris: 40, 46, 47. National Cycle Museum, Lincoln: 105(tr, b). National Motor Museum, Beaulieu: 95. The National Trust: 41 Michael Freeman, 48, 67 Charlie Waite, 71(cr) Charlie Waite. Peter Newarks Wester Americana: 57. Ian O'Leary: 48/9, 50/1, 52/3, 54/5, 72/3. O'Shea Gallery, London: 77(t). Peter Reilly: 52/3, 69(t, b). Shelburne Museum, Shelburne, Vermont: 66. Duncan Smith: 6, 56, 65/7, 58/9, 60/1, 62/3, 64, 64/5. Sotheby's: 35(bl, br). Victoria & Albert Museum, London: 76. Elizabeth Whiting & Associates: 71(bl), 83, 84(b), 87(t). Yale University Art Gallery, Bequest of Stephen Carlton Clark BA, 1903: 65.

Some of this material has previously appeared in the partwork Times Past.